CW00558006

STAFFORD
TO
WELLINGTON

Vic Mitchell and Keith Smith

MP Middleton Press

Front cover: Wellington received a direct service to London from 2008 to 2011, courtesy of the Wrexham & Shropshire Railway. One of the three weekday trains is seen on 6th August 2008, with no. 67028 leading. It is the 11.10 Wrexham to Marylebone, with no. 67019 on the rear. (M.J.Stretton)

Back cover upper: The 1903 Railway Clearing House map reveals the eastern limit of the joint lines. The Coalport branch was further east.

Back cover lower: Class 4MT 2-6-4T no. 42104 enters Trench Crossing station on 5th September 1964. Trench was the name of a nearby village. (Colour-Rail.com)

Published May 2014

ISBN 978 1 908174 59 8

© Middleton Press, 2014

Design Deborah Esher

Published by
*   Middleton Press*
*   Easebourne Lane*
*   Midhurst*
*   West Sussex*
*   GU29 9AZ*
Tel: 01730 813169
Fax: 01730 812601
Email: info@middletonpress.co.uk
www.middletonpress.co.uk

Printed in the United Kingdom by Henry Ling Limited, at the Dorset Press, Dorchester, DT1 1HD

INDEX

ACKNOWLEDGEMENTS

We are very grateful for the assistance received from many of those mentioned in the credits also to A.R.Carder, J.P.McCrickard, G.Croughton, M.J.Dodd, G.Gartside, S.C.Jenkins, N.Langridge, B.Lewis, I.Pell, Mr D. and Dr S.Salter, Dr M. Thompson and in particular, our always supportive wives, Barbara Mitchell and Janet Smith.

I. The 1947 Railway Clearing House diagram.

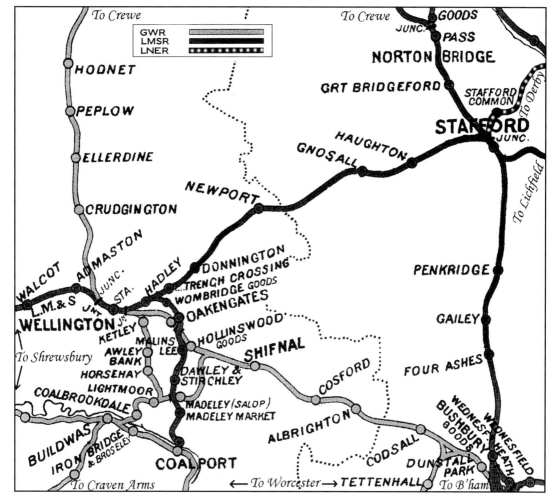

GEOGRAPHICAL SETTING

The area south of Wellington is deemed to be the cradle of the Industrial Revolution and the Coalport branch served the eastern part of it. Its existence here was due to the complex geology, which resulted in close outcrops of coal and iron ore. The area is in close proximity to the River Severn, which was ideal for transport.

The branch passes over a flat topped ridge, with steep gradients passing through Madeley and Oakengates, each side of the high ground. The area is now totally urbanised and has the name of Telford, in memory of the talented civil engineer. The Shropshire Union Canal ran north of Wellington, through Newport, to join its main route.

The first few miles of our journey are over sandstones. The watercourses of this area flow into the River Sow near Stafford. The route of the railway between Newport and Stafford has become The Way for the Millennium, while some lengths near Donnington have been adapted for the A518.

The maps are to the scale of 25ins to 1 mile with north at the top, unless otherwise indicated.

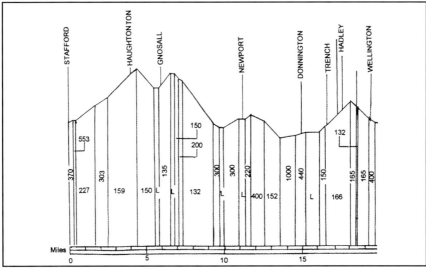

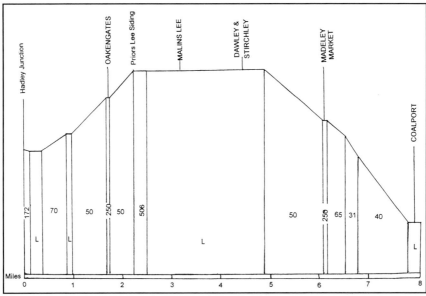

II. The northern two miles of the route of the Coalport branch are now under the dual carriageway of the A442, which forms the Telford bypass. The southern five miles form part of the 14-mile Silkin Way for cyclists and walkers, but with minor deviations. The route south of Dawley & Stirchley lost its freight service on 5th December 1960 and the northern part was closed completely on 6th July 1964. This 1946 extract is at about 1½ ins to 1 mile.

Part I of the DVD *Steaming through Shropshire* includes our route and others in the north of the county. This is available from Middleton Press.

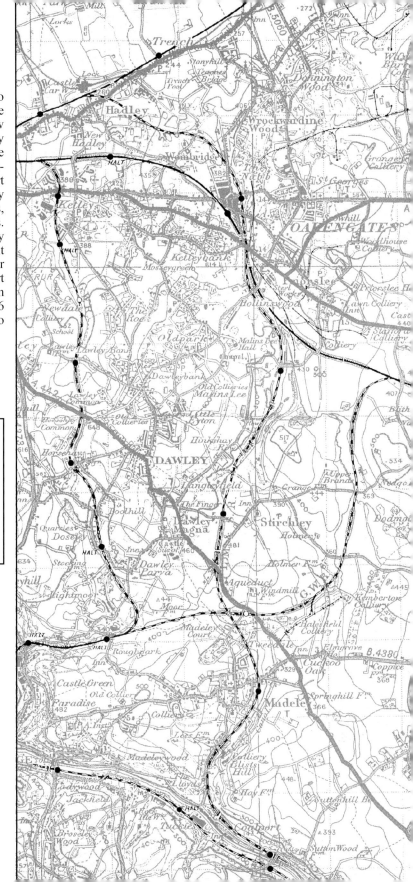

HISTORICAL BACKGROUND

The first route in the area was that of the Grand Junction Railway, which opened in 1837. It ran from Birmingham, close to Wolverhampton, through Stafford and on to Crewe, terminating at Warrington. It became a constituent of the London & North Western Railway upon this being formed in 1846.

The Shropshire Union Railway Act was passed on 3rd August 1846, it authorising a line between Shrewsbury and Stafford. It absorbed the Shrewsbury Canal Company and became known as the Shropshire Union Railway & Canal Company. The section west of Wellington was a joint venture with the Shrewsbury & Birmingham Railway, which became part of the Great Western Railway in 1854.

The Wellington-Stafford section was completed by the SUR&CR and the entire route between Shrewsbury and Stafford opened on 1st June 1849. However, the part west of Wellington became jointly owned by the LNWR and the GWR in 1854. See the back cover diagram.

Wellington was served from the south from 1857 by the Wellington & Severn Junction Railway. This became part of the GWR in 1892 and closed in 1964. The route from the north was opened by the GWR in 1867 and was in use until 1967. The former ran from Much Wenlock and the latter began at Market Drayton.

The route from Stafford remained in SUR&CR ownership until 1923, although operated by the LNWR. The latter then became part of the new London Midland & Scottish Railway. This formed the London Midland Region of British Railways upon nationalisation in 1948, but Wellington remained in the Western Region until 1st June 1963.

The route closed to passengers on 7th September 1964, but was open for through trains until 1st August 1966. The section north of Newport was in use for freight until 1968, as was the southern two miles until 28th March 1991, but it reopened on 29th October 2008 to Donnington.

Coalport Branch

The line was opened by the LNWR on 10th June 1861 and was closed to passengers on 2nd June 1951, freight continuing until 6th July 1964, except at the southern end.

July 1878

Mls	Fares.				*frm. Wor'ster,p.17*	gov	aft	aft	ait	*From Crewe, p. 17.*	gov	aft	aft	a
	1 cl.	2 cl.	3 cl.											
—					Coalport .... dep	7 30	1215	5 0	6 45	Wellington .. dep	1045	1 45	6 0	8 50
1¼	6 0	4 0	2	Madeley Market 17	7 38	1223	5 11	6 53	Hadley	1050	1 50	6 5	8 55
3½	0 8 0	6 0	3	Stirchley 1	7 45	1230	5 20	7 0	Oakengates......	11 1	2 1	6 15	9 6
4½	0 9 0	6 0	4½	Malins Lee	7 50	1235	5 25	7 5	Malins Lee	11 7	2 7	6 20	9 13
6¼	1 0 0	9 0	6	Oakengates 20 ..	7 57	1241	5 32	7 12	Stirchley 1	1112	2 12	6 25	9 17
8½	1 4 1	0 0	8	Hadley [*and above*	8 5	1250	5 40	7 18	Madeley Market 17	1117	2 18	6 32	9 23
9½	1 9 1	3 0	9	Wellington 17, arr	8 10	1255	5 45	7 25	Coalport 17 ..arr	1125	2 25	6 37	9 30

a Runs 10 minutes later on Saturdays. 1, Station for Dawley.

COALPORT BRANCH.—L. & N. W. [District Man., J. Entwistle.

April 1880

Mls	Fares.				*frm. Wor'ster,p.24*	mrn	aft	aft	aft	*frm Crewe, p. 24*	mrn	aft	aft	a
	1 cl.	2 cl.	3 cl.											
—					Coalport .... dep	7 30	1215	5 0	6 45	Wellington dep	1045	1 35	6 0	8 50
1¼	0 6 0	4 0	2	Madeley Market 24	7 38	1223	5 11	6 53	Hadley	1050	1 40	6 5	8 55
3½	0 8 0	6 0	3	Stirchley 1	7 45	1230	5 20	7 0	Oakengates....	11 1	1 51	6 15	9 6
4½	0 9 0	6 0	4½	Malins Lee	7 50	1235	5 25	7 5	Malins Lee	11 7	1 57	6 20	9 13
6½	1 0 0	9 0	6	Oakengates 20 ..	7 57	1241	5 32	7 12	Stirchley 1	1112	2 2	6 25	9 17
8½	1 4 1	0 0	8	Hadley [*and above*	8 5	1250	5 40	7 18	Madely Markt 24	1117	2 8	6 32	9 23
9½	1 9 1	3 0	9	Wellington 24, arr	8 10	1255	5 45	7 25	Coalport 24 arr	1125	2 15	6 37	9 30

a Runs 15 minutes later on Saturdays. 1, Station for Dawley.

PASSENGER SERVICES

These notes refer to up trains, these running to Stafford, and the figures in brackets give the number of trains on Sundays. Only those running the full length of the route are mentioned. However, it is worth noting that there was one train to Stafford starting at Newport every morning between 6.20 and 7.09 for over 70 years. These are shown on some of the sample tables, as are some of the through trains, Aberystwyth to Euston being one of the longest.

The initial frequency was just 3 (2), but by 1878 it had grown to 7 (3). In 1909 and 1939 it was 12 (2 and 5). By 1948 and also the final complete year it was 9 (2). In the last years, trains called at all stations, but the extracts show many interesting semi-fast through trains.

Coalport Branch

No Sunday trains have been found. The opening service was 3 (plus 1 on Thursdays) and it was 4 by 1880. In 1905 the figure was 5 (plus 2 on Saturdays). It dropped to 4 in wartime in 1943 and rose to 6 in 1948. The final timetable in 1951 offered 4 (plus 1 on Thursdays and 2 on Saturdays). All terminated at Wellington.

July 1878

April 1880

STAFFORD, NEWPORT, WELLINGTON, SHREWSBURY, and WELSHPOOL.—London and North Western and Great Western.

Joint Supt., John Williams. L. & N. W. Co.'s Traffic Supt., J. L. White Shrewsbury.

Miles.	Up.	Week Days.																									Sundays.				
		mrn	mrn	mrn	mrn	mrn	mrn	mrn	mrn	mrn	mrn	aft	aft	aft	aft	aft	aft	aft	aft	aft	aft	aft					mrn	mrn	aft	aft	aft
	459 Aberystwyth ....dep.	....	....	....	....	....	....	....	8u0	....	....	....	....	....	....	1u10	....	....	....	....	3 55	6 25	....	....	....	....	....	....	....	....	6 25
	Welshpool ....dep.	....	....	....	....	....	9 0	....	1042	....	1135	....	....	....	....	3 35	....	....	....	....	6 45	9 5	....	....	....	....	....	9 30	....	....	9 5
2¾	Buttington	....	....	....	....	....	9 5	....	....	....	1140	....	....	....	....	3 40	....	....	....	....	6 50	9 11	....	....	....	....	....	9 35	....	....	9 11
5¾	Middletown	....	....	....	....	....	9 12	....	....	....	1147	....	....	....	....	3 48	....	....	....	....	6 58	9 18	....	....	....	....	....	9 43	....	....	9 18
8¾	Westbury	....	....	....	....	....	9 17	....	....	....	1152	....	....	....	....	3 54	....	....	....	....	7 3	9 24	....	....	....	....	....	9 49	....	....	9 24
12¼	Yockleton	....	....	....	....	....	9 25	....	....	....	12 0	....	....	....	....	4 0	....	....	....	....	7 10	f	....	....	....	....	....	9 57	....	....	9 31
14¾	Hanwood 470 ....[452	....	....	....	....	....	9 32	....	....	....	12 7	....	....	....	....	4 8	....	....	....	....	7 17	9 38	....	....	....	....	....	10 5	....	....	9 38
19¾	Shrewsbury (Gen.) 76, 450 arr.	....	....	....	....	....	9 45	....	1118	....	1220	....	....	....	....	4 20	....	....	....	....	7 30	9 50	....	....	....	....	....	1020	....	....	9 50
62	77 Birmingham (Snow H.). arr.	....	....	....	....	....	1112	....	1 7	....	2 38	....	....	....	....	5 40	....	....	....	....	1025	....	....	....	....	....	....	1 36	....	....	....
191¼	77 London (Paddington).. "	....	....	....	....	....	2 8	....	5 14	....	5 20	....	....	....	....	8 50	....	....	....	....	....	....	....	....	....	....	....	5 48	....	....	....
—	Shrewsbury ....dep.	7 5	....	7 40	9 20	10 0	1010	1020	1140	1145	1235	2 40	2 45	3 10	....	....	4 30	4 50	5 25	5 43	8 0	10 8	....	....	....	....	8 35	1140	4 25	7 5	10 8
23½	Upton Magna	7 14	....	c	9 28	....	....	1028	....	1153	....	....	2 53	....	....	....	....	....	5 33	....	8 8	....	....	....	....	....	8 42	1148	4 33	7 13	....
26	Walcot	7 21	....	c	9 34	....	....	1034	....	1159	....	....	2 59	....	....	....	....	....	5 39	....	8 15	....	....	....	....	....	8 48	1154	4 39	7 19	....
28½	Admaston	7 26	....	....	9 39	....	....	1039	....	12 4	....	....	3 4	....	....	....	....	....	5 44	....	8 22	....	....	....	....	....	8 54	....	4 44	7 24	....
30¼	Wellington 98, 428	7 30	....	7 59	9 43	1015	1026	1043	1158	1211	1255	2 56	3 8	3 27	3 35	....	4 45	5 11	5 48	5 59	8 28	1026	....	....	....	....	9 0	12 2	4 49	7 28	1026
31¼	Hadley	....	....	8 3	....	....	....	....	....	1216	....	....	....	....	3 40	....	....	....	....	....	8 33	....	....	....	....	....	....	....	4 54	....	....
32¼	Trench Crossing	....	....	8 6	....	....	....	....	....	1220	....	3 0	....	....	3 44	....	....	....	....	6 5	8 37	....	....	....	....	....	....	....	4 58	....	....
34	Donnington	....	....	8 10	....	....	1032	....	....	1224	....	3 6	....	....	3 48	....	....	5 17	....	6 9	8 40	....	....	....	....	....	....	....	5 1	....	....
37¼	Newport	....	7 9	8 16	....	....	1039	....	....	1230	1 6	3 13	....	....	3 55	....	....	5 25	....	6 16	8 48	1037	....	....	....	....	....	....	5 8	....	1037
42¾	Gnosall	....	7 18	8 27	....	....	1048	....	....	1242	....	3 23	....	....	4 7	....	....	....	....	6 27	9 0	....	....	....	....	....	....	....	5 23	....	....
45	Haughton.....[439, 443, 525	....	7 30	8 33	....	....	....	....	....	1251	....	....	....	....	4 15	....	....	....	....	6 36	9 10	....	....	....	....	....	....	....	5 35	....	....
49	Stafford 369, 403, 411, arr.	....	7 44	8 42	....	....	11 0	....	1225	1 0	1 25	3 33	....	3 53	4 25	....	....	5 45	....	6 46	9 20	1055	....	....	....	....	....	....	5 45	....	1055
77¼	443 Birmingham (New St.) arr.	....	9 16	9 59	....	....	1241	....	1 57	....	2 55	....	....	4 52	5 57	....	....	7 24	....	7 55	1135	2 33	....	....	....	....	....	....	7 30	....	2 33
182¾	411 London (Euston)...... "	....	g 1050	12 0	....	....	1 40	....	3u15	4 20	5 15	....	....	7n0	....	....	....	8u50	....	1115	....	3i50	....	....	....	....	....	....	9 0	....	3i50

b Passengers travel in slip carriage.
c Stops to take up for Stafford and beyond on giving notice at Station.
d Except Sunday nights.
f Stops to set down on notice being given to the Guard.
g Except Mondays.
i 1st and 3rd class.
n Via Birmingham.
o Leaves at 6 55 aft. on Saturdays, via Birmingham.
s Saturdays only.
t Leaves at 10 15 aft. on Sundays.
u Through Carriages to and from Aberystwyth.
* Station for Llanfair.

March 1909

August 1939

STAFFORD, WELLINGTON, SHREWSBURY, and WELSHPOOL

Miles from Welshpool	Up	Week Days																										Sundays					
		mrn	mrn	mn	mrn	mrn	mn	mrn	mrn	mrn	aft	mrn	S	E	aft	aft	aft	aft	aft	aft	aft	aft	aft	aft	aft Except Weds. and Sats.	aft Wednesdays only	aft Saturdays only.	mrn	aft	aft	aft	aft	aft
	144 Barmouth ....dep.	..	..	..	..	..	..	..	7 10	B	..	..	9 40	9 40	..		10r40	1220	Z	..	223	..	..	5 43				..	..	..	2 50	..	..
	144 Aberystwyth ..... "	..	..	..	..	..	..	..	7 30	..	..	9u15	10 15	1045	..	..	12 5	1 0	2 35	..	250	..	..	6 10				..	..	..	3 30	..	..
	Welshpool ....dep	..	..	..	..	..	845	..	10 0	..	..	1130	12 40	1250	..	..	2 40	3 20	5 5	..	530	..	..	8 50				..	..	..	5 34	..	..
	142 Oswestry ....dep.	..	..	..	..	..	820	..	..	..	..	1055	..	..	..	..	1F50	2F32	3F0	..	3 0	..	..	7F55				..	..	..	4U5	..	..
2¼	Buttington	..	..	..	..	..	852	..	..	..	..	1135	..	..	..	..	2 45	..	..	..	535	..	..	..				..	..	..	..	..	..
5¼	Breidden ¶	..	..	..	..	..	9 1	..	..	..	..	1143	..	..	..	..	2 54	3 35	..	..	543	..	..	9 4				..	..	..	..	..	..
8¼	Westbury	..	..	..	..	..	912	..	..	..	..	1153	Yy	Yy	..	..	3 3	3 46	..	..	554	..	..	9 13				..	..	..	..	..	..
12½	Yockleton	..	..	..	..	..	920	..	..	..	..	12 0	..	..	..	..	3 10	..	..	..	6 1	..	..	9 21				..	..	..	..	..	..
15	Hanwood 492	..	..	..	..	..	926	..	..	..	..	12 6	..	..	..	..	3 15	..	..	..	6 6	..	..	Aa				..	..	..	..	..	..
19¼	Shrewsbury (Gen) 108, 488, 490 arr.	..	..	..	..	..	938	..	1038	..	..	1216	1 18	1 31	..	..	3 25	4 11	..	..	618	..	..	9 35		..		..	..	..	6 9	..	..
	dep.	..	6 53	7 0	7 55	9 10	943	1020	11 0	1140	1214	1 0	1 37	..	239	313	3 30	4 50	..	5§56	626	8 5	812	9 55	1050	1050	1050	8 55	1245	4 20	6 25	7 28	9 10
23½	Upton Magna	..	7 0	7 8	..	9 17	..	1027	11 7	..	1221	1 7	..	..	..	320	3 38	..	..	6§3	..	8 12	819	10S3	..	..	1057	..	..	..	..	7 37	..
26	Walcot	..	7 4	714	..	9 21	..	..	1111	..	1225	1 11	..	..	..	324	3 43	..	..	6§7	..	..	823	10S9	..	..	11 2	..	..	..	..	7 42	..
28½	Admaston	..	7 9	720	..	9 26	..	..	1116	..	1230	1 16	..	..	..	329	3 49	..	..	6§12	..	..	828	10S14	..	..	11 7	..	..	..	..	..	..
30½	Wellington 112, 129, 138, 484 arr.	..	7 14	728	8 10	9 30	959	1039	1120	1155	1234	1 20	1 52	..	254	333	3 55	5 8	6 2	6§16	640	8 24	835	10l10	11 5	11 5	1111	9 12	1 4	4 35	6 41	7 49	9 28
	dep.	6A45	7 21	..	8 13	..	..	1040	..	1157	1237	..	1 55	..	2 6	336	..	5 10	..	6§18	..	8 29	..	10 21	11 7	11 7	1113	1049	1 35	4 37	..	8 0	1015
31½	Hadley	6A48	7 24	..	8 16	..	..	1043	..	..	1240	..	1 58	..	25	339	..	5 13	..	6§21	..	8 32	..	10 25	..	..	1116	1052	1 38	4 40	..	8 3	1018
32½	Trench Crossing	6A51	7 27	..	8 19	..	..	1046	..	..	1243	..	2 1	..	3 2	342	..	5 16	..	6§24	..	8 35	..	10 28	..	..	1119	1055	1 41	4 43	..	8 6	1021
34	Donnington	6A55	7 31	..	8 23	..	..	1050	..	..	1247	..	2 5	..	3 6	346	..	5 20	..	6§28	..	8 39	..	10 32	..	1114	1123	1059	1 45	4 47	..	8 10	1025
37½	Newport	7 4	7 40	..	8 30	..	..	1057	..	1211	1254	..	2 12	..	313	353	..	5 27	..	6§35	..	8 46	..	10 39	1119	1121	1130	11 6	1 52	4 54	..	8 17	1032
42¼	Gnosall	7 13	7 48	..	8 40	..	..	11 7	..	..	1 3	..	2 21	..	322	4 2	..	5 36	..	6§44	..	8 56	..	10 49	..	..	..	1116	2 2	5 4	..	8 27	1042
45	Haughton [483, 532, 902	7 18	7 53	..	8 45	..	..	1112	..	..	1 8	..	2 26	..	327	4 7	..	5 41	..	6§49	..	9 1	..	10 54	..	..	..	..	..	..	..	..	..
49	Stafford 413, 425, 478 arr	7 25	8 0	..	8 52	..	..	1120	..	1232	1 16	..	2 35	..	337	415	..	5 49	..	7§1	..	9 8	..	11 2	1136	1138	1147	1126	2 12	5 14	..	8 44	1052
77½	478 Birmingham (N.St) arr.	....	9 3	..	1039	..	..	1 5	..	1 57	2L54	..	3 53	..	..	525	..	6a55	..	8†25	..	1141	..	..	4 50	4 50	7T13	1 9	3 55	7 20	..	10 8	6 16
182½	425 London (Euston).. "	..	1050	..	1242	..	..	2 41	..	3n55	5V37	..	5 20	..	..	7 5	..	9b0	..	10§40	..	3w35	..	..	5p53	5 53	5 42	2 35	8O15	9 5	..	3 30	5 27

A TC London (E) to Central Wales Spas & Swansea (Vic) pp 472 A Mons only **Aa** Sets down from Welshpool or beyond on notice being given to Guard at Welshpool
a Arr 7 2 aft Sats **B** TC Swansea (Vic) to London (E) page 493 B Except Sun ngts *b* Arr 9 6 aft Sats (9 15 aft 5th Aug 16th and 23rd Sept) O Via Birmingham
c Dep 11 5 mrn Sats D Arr 1 45 aft Sats until 9th Sept *d* Dep 10 55 mrn Sats until 9th Sept **E** or E Except Sats F Via Welshpool H Except Mons *h* On 10th, 17th, 24th and 31st August via Welshpool J Arr 10 3 mrn Weds K Dep 5 10 aft Sats 8th to 29th July and 19th Aug to 23rd Sept *k* Arr 8 55 aft on Sats (5 20 aft on 16th and 23rd Sept) L Arr 2 41 aft Sats *l* 8 mins later on Sats *n* Arr 3 27 aft Sats 29th July to 19th Aug P Sats only, not after 2nd Sept, Via Welshpool
p Arr 3 30 mrn Sats R Arr 11 56 mrn Sats until 2nd Sept, via Welshpool *r* Not after 9th Sept Dep 11 43 mrn on Sats to 2nd Sept **S** or S Sats only

T Arr 4 45 Sun morns 30th July to 17th Sept *t* Dep 7 35 mrn on 24th and 31st July, 14th, 21st and 28th Aug TC Through Carriage U Road Motor, via Gobowen
u Sats, not after 2nd Sept V Arr 4 24 aft Sats 12th Aug to 2nd Sept & 4 30 aft other Sats *v* Dep 1 35 mrn 12th, 19th & 26th Aug *w* Via Birmingham. Arr 3 18 mrn Sats

WELSHPOOL, SHREWSBURY, WELLINGTON, and STAFFORD

Week Days

Miles from Welshpool		a.m	a.m	a.m	a.m	a.m	a.m	a.m	a.m	a.m	a.m	a.m	a.m	a.m	p.m E	p.m S	a.m	p.m	p.m	p.m	non	p.m
	Barmouth ....dep	..	..	..	..	..	..	..	..	..	..	..	..	7 11	..	..	9 35	..	..	..	..	..
	Aberystwyth....... "	..	..	..	..	..	..	5U35	..	..	..	..	..	7 40	..	..	10 0	..	..	..	12 0	..
	Welshpool............dep	..	..	..	..	..	..	8 15	..	..	..	..	..	1035	..	..	1240	..	..	..	2 30	..
	Oswestry ....dep	..	..	..	..	..	..	4F5	..	..	..	..	..	8 20	..	..	1050	..	..	..	..	..
2¾	Buttington...............	..	..	..	..	..	..	8 21	..	..	..	..	..	1041	..	..	1246	..	..	..	2 36	..
5¾	Breidden ¶	..	..	..	..	..	..	8 30	..	..	..	..	..	1048	..	..	1254	..	..	..	2 43	..
8¾	Westbury	..	..	..	..	..	..	8 42	..	..	..	..	..	1059	..	..	1 4	..	..	..	2 52	..
12¼	Yockleton	..	..	..	..	..	..	8 50	..	..	..	..	..	11 6	..	..	1 11	..	..	..	..	..
15	Hanwood	..	..	..	..	..	..	8 57	..	..	..	..	..	1113	..	..	1 17	..	..	..	3 7	..
19¾	**Shrewsbury**......... arr	..	..	..	..	..	..	9 8	..	..	..	..	..	1126	..	..	1 28	..	..	..	3 18	..
	dep	6 35	..	7 25	7 55	8 0	8 37	..	9 30	1038	1050	1115	1123	..	1220	1220	..	1 45	2 15	3 10	..	3 30
23⅓	Upton Magna.............	6 43	..	..	..	8 7	..	..	..	..	1057	..	1130	..	1226	1226	..	..	..	3 17	..	..
26	Walcot..................	6 48	..	..	..	8 12	..	..	..	..	11 2	..	1135	..	1231	1231	..	..	..	3 22	..	..
28½	Admaston	6 53	..	..	..	8 16	..	..	..	..	11 7	..	1140	..	1236	1236	..	..	..	3 27	..	..
30¼	**Wellington**.......... arr	6 57	..	7 39	8 10	8 21	8 55	..	9 46	1055	1112	1135	1145	..	1241	1241	..	1 59	2 31	3 32	..	3 45
	dep	▬	7 5	..	8 14	..	..	..	..	..	..	..	1147	..	1243	1243	..	..	..	3 38	..	..
31½	Hadley..................	Stop	7 10	..	8 17	..	..	..	..	..	..	..	1150	..	..	1247	..	..	..	3 41	..	..
32¾	Trench Crossing..........	..	7 14	..	8 20	..	..	..	..	..	..	..	1153	..	..	1250	..	..	..	3 44	..	..
34	Donnington	..	7 21	..	8 28	..	..	..	..	..	..	..	1159	..	1252	1256	..	..	..	3 50	..	..
37½	Newport..................	7 0	7 29	..	8 37	..	..	..	..	..	..	..	12 6	..	1259	1 3	..	..	..	3 57	..	..
42¾	Gnosall	7 9	7 39	..	8 47	..	..	..	..	..	..	..	1216	..	..	..	..	..	..	4 7	..	..
45	Haughton	7 14	7 44	..	8 52	..	..	..	..	..	..	..	1221	..	..	..	..	..	..	4 12	..	..
49	**Stafford** ....arr	7 22	7 52	..	9 0	..	..	..	..	..	..	..	1230	..	1 26	1 26	..	..	..	4 23	..	..
77¾	76 Birmingham(NewSt.)arr	..	9 16	..	1121	..	..	..	..	..	..	..	..	..	2 55	2 55	..	..	..	5 55	..	..
182½	50 London (Euston).... "	..	1125	..	1250	..	..	..	..	..	..	..	3 50	..	4 35	4 35	..	..	..	8 25	..	..

Week Days—*continued* / **Sundays**

	Week Days p.m	p.m	p.m S	p.m	p.m	p.m	p.m	p.m	p.m	p.m	p.m S	p.m E	p.m		Sundays a.m	a.m	a.m	non	p.m	p.m	p.m	p.m
Barmouth ....dep	1220	..	..	..	..	2 0	..	..	5 30	..	..	..	..	..	..	..	..	..	..	..	..	..
Aberystwyth ...... "	1250	..	..	..	..	2 30	..	..	6 0	..	..	..	..	..	..	..	..	..	..	..	..	..
Welshpool.............dep	3 15	..	..	..	..	5 20	..	..	8 50	..	..	..	..	..	..	..	..	..	..	..	..	..
Oswestry ....dep	..	..	..	..	..	3 5	..	..	8 5	..	..	..	..	..	..	..	..	..	..	..	..	..
Buttington...............	..	..	..	..	..	5 26	..	..	8 56	..	..	..	..	..	..	..	..	..	..	..	..	..
Breidden ¶	3 27	..	..	..	..	5 34	..	..	9 4	..	..	..	..	..	..	..	..	..	..	..	..	..
Westbury	3 37	..	..	..	..	5 44	..	..	9 14	..	..	..	..	..	..	..	..	..	..	..	..	..
Yockleton...............	3 45	..	..	..	..	5 51	..	..	9 21	..	..	..	..	..	..	..	..	..	..	..	..	..
Hanwood	3 54	..	..	..	..	5 57	..	..	9 27	..	..	..	..	..	..	..	..	..	..	..	..	..
Shrewsbury......... arr	4 10	..	Third class only	..	..	6 8	..	..	9 36	..	..	..	..	..	..	..	..	..	..	..	..	..
dep	..	4 35		5 10	5 50	..	6 28	8 28	▬	..	1010	1015	1125	..	8 0	10 3	..	12 0	5 12	7 35	..	9 12
Upton Magna.............	..	..		5 17	5 56	..	..	8 37	Stop	..	1018	..	..	..	..	..	..	12 7	..	7 43	..	..
Walcot..................	..	..		5 22	6 1	..	..	8 41	..	..	1023	..	..	..	..	..	..	1211	..	7 47	..	..
Admaston...............	..	..		5 28	6 6	..	..	8 46	..	..	1029	..	..	..	..	..	..	..	..	..	..	..
Wellington .... arr	..	4 52		5 33	6 11	..	6 45	8 51	p.m	..	1034	1029	1140	..	8 14	1024	..	1219	5 32	7 55	..	9 23
dep	..	..	5 20	..	6 15	..	..	..	9 5	10Y15	..	..	1145	..	..	..	1140	..	..	..	8 5	..
Hadley..................	..	..	5 24	..	6 19	..	..	..	9 8	10Y19	..	..	..	..	..	..	1143	..	..	..	8 9	..
Trench Crossing..........	..	..	5 28	..	6 22	..	..	..	9 11	10Y22	..	..	..	..	..	..	1146	..	..	..	8 12	..
Donnington	..	..	5 32	..	6 30	..	..	..	9 18	10Y27	..	..	..	..	..	..	1150	..	..	..	8 16	..
Newport..................	..	..	5 39	..	6 38	..	..	..	9 25	10Y36	..	..	..	..	..	..	1157	..	..	..	8 23	..
Gnosall..................	..	..	..	..	6 49	..	..	..	9 35	10Y46	..	..	..	..	..	..	12 7	..	..	..	8 33	..
Haughton................	..	..	..	..	6 54	..	..	..	9 40	..	..	..	..	..	..	..	..	..	..	..	..	..
Stafford .... arr	..	..	..	..	7 3	..	..	..	9 48	10Y58	..	..	1213	..	..	..	1222	..	..	..	8 45	..
76 Birmingham(NewSt.)arr	..	..	..	..	9 15	..	..	..	1125	..	..	..	5B25	..	..	..	2 10	..	..	..	1020	..
50 London (Euston).... "	..	..	..	..	1120	..	..	..	..	..	..	..	6a15	..	..	..	6 20	..	..	..	4a25	..

a a.m B Except Mondays. On Sundays arr. 7 55 a.m E or E Except Saturdays F Via Welshpool

S Saturdays only U Mondays only Y Runs 5 mins. later on Saturdays

¶ "Halt" at Plas-y-Court between Breidden and Westbury

September 1948

June 1951

WELLINGTON AND COALPORT — Weekdays only.

Miles.		a.m.	ThSO a.m.	p.m.	p.m.	p.m.	SO p.m.
0	**Wellington P** ....dep.	8 4	10 2	1 35	3 53	6 30	9 15
1¼	**Hadley P**	8 10	10 6	1 39	3 57	6 35	9 19
3¼	Oakengates......................	8 18	10 14	1 47	4 6	6 44	9 27
4¾	Malins Lee	8 23	10 19	1 52	4 11	6 49	9 32
6	Dawley & Stirchley	8 27	10 23	1 56	4 16	6 53	9 36
7¼	Madeley Market	8 32	10 28	2 1	4 21	6 58	9 41
9¼	**Coalport** .... arr.	8 37	10 33	2 6	4 26	7 3	9 46

Miles.		a.m.	a.m.	ThO a.m.	SO a.m.	p.m.	p.m.	SO p.m.
0	**Coalport** ....dep.	6 17	8 50	11 23	11 57	2 35	4 35	7 40
2	Madeley Market	6 23	8 56	11 29	12 3	2 41	4 41	7 46
3¼	Dawley & Stirchley	6 28	9 1	11 34	12 8	2 46	4 46	7 51
4¾	Malins Lee	6 32	9 5	11 38	12 12	2 50	4 50	7 55
6¼	Oakengates......................	6 36	9 9	11 42	12 16	2 55	4 55	8 0
8¼	**Hadley P**	6 42	9 15	11 48	12 22	3 1	5 4	8 6
9¼	**Wellington P** .... arr.	6 49	9 20	11 55	12 27	3 6	5 9	8 13

P—For additional trains between Wellington and Hadley, see table 75.
SO—Saturdays only.

ThO—Thursdays only.
ThX—Thursdays excepted.
ThSO—Thursdays and Saturdays only.

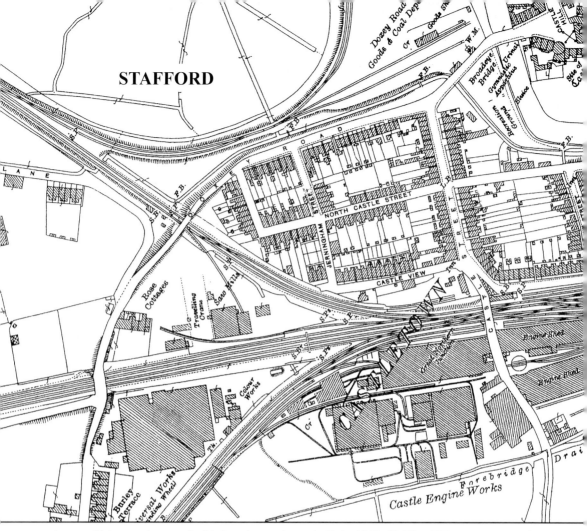

STAFFORD

1.   This was the town's third station and was built in 1861-62. The GJR structure was in use in 1837-44. The second one was on the London side of the present one. (J.K.Williams coll.)

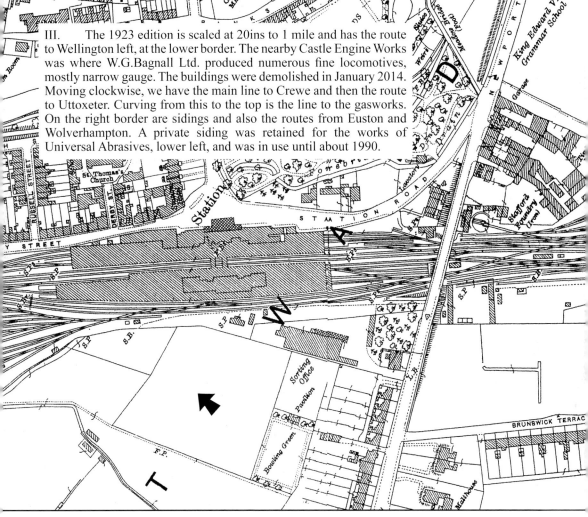

III.   The 1923 edition is scaled at 20ins to 1 mile and has the route to Wellington left, at the lower border. The nearby Castle Engine Works was where W.G.Bagnall Ltd. produced numerous fine locomotives, mostly narrow gauge. The buildings were demolished in January 2014. Moving clockwise, we have the main line to Crewe and then the route to Uttoxeter. Curving from this to the top is the line to the gasworks. On the right border are sidings and also the routes from Euston and Wolverhampton. A private siding was retained for the works of Universal Abrasives, lower left, and was in use until about 1990.

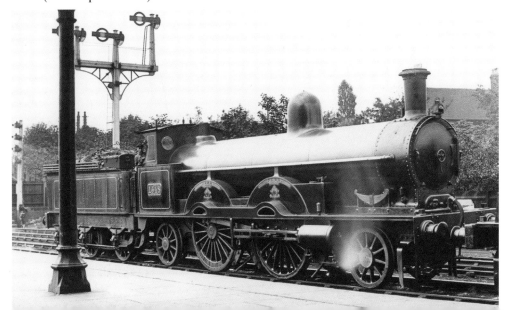

2.   Probably a glass plate was used to make this splendid record of no. 1548 *John Penn* in about 1905. The 2-2-2-2 had an inside cylinder, as well as two outside ones. It is a John Hick class. (R.S.Carpenter coll.)

3.　　　Staff members were often used to enhance postcard views. This one shows that the through lines did not have a roof over them, there being train sheds each side of them. (P.Laming coll.)

4.　　　The engine sheds are left of centre on the map and are seen from the station in 1925. The first sheds were south of the station. The two seen date from 1852 and 1861; they had four and six roads respectively. There was a fleet of 20 engines here in 1855, all with names. (R.M.Casserley coll.)

5.   Great Northern Junction is just beyond Castle Street bridge, which is in the distance. The original SUR engine shed had been to the left of the former. This view is from 23rd August 1948 and includes a closer view of the same signal gantry, seen in picture 4. (H.C.Casserley)

6.   A southward view from 1949 has the through roads to the left of the water column and gloom elsewhere. The intricate structures were to last until 1960. (Stations UK)

7.　　Parcel vans and a container form part of a down train, while parcels litter the up side, sometime in 1949. Much of the glazing had been removed by that time. (Stations UK)

8.　　The north end is seen in 1958, when the signalling was in transition. The platforms on the right were used by local trains to Wellington. The island platform was created in the 1880s. (Stations UK)

9. No. 5 Box was north of the station and is seen on 13th June 1957, with No. 2 shed behind it. The box had 150 levers and opened on 18th February 1952. It was the only one of the six still to be in use in 2014. (H.F.Wheeller/R.S.Carpenter coll.)

10. A glimpse inside Bagnall's new erecting shop in 1956 includes an overhead travelling crane and part of an export order for 3ft 6ins gauge diesel locomotives. The firm existed from 1887 to 1961. (A.Dudman.coll.)

11.   The six-road shed was known as No. 2 and had this roof from 1947. The code 5C was applied from 1948 until closure in 1965, when its allocation was just nine locomotives. It had been 24 in 1959. Seen on 25th July 1964 is BR class 5 4-6-0 no. 73025. (J.M.Tolson/F.Hornby coll.)

12.   We have a northward view from 11th June 1973 to show the results of the rebuilding. The official opening was on 31st December 1962. The old order was down slow, down fast, up fast, up goods. The new order became down slow, up slow, down fast, up fast, south of the station. The new design gave five through platforms, instead of three. There was no No. 2. The bay lines on the right were later reduced to one. (D.A.Thompson)

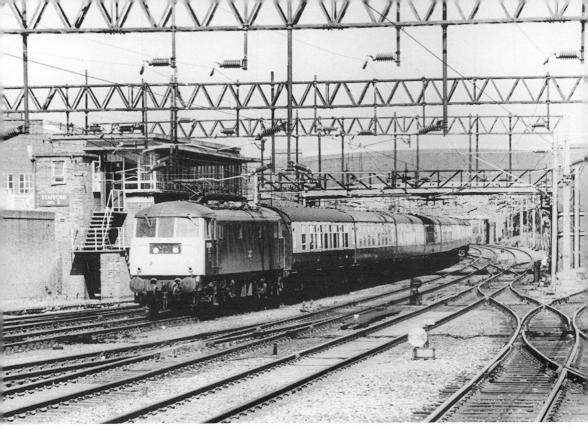

13.   The route between Lichfield and Crewe was electrified in 1963 and electric traction is seen in action on 29th July 1978, as no. 81014 speeds south near No. 5 Box, with a Manchester to Weymouth express. (T.Heavyside)

Other views of this station and the adjacent junctions are to be found in the *Rugby to Stafford* and the *Stafford to Chester* albums.

STAFFORD.

A telegraph station.

HOTELS.—Swan; Vine; Grand Junction.

MARKET DAY.—Saturday.

FAIRS.—April, May, June, and October, annually.

BANKERS.—Stevenson, Salt, and Co.; Branch of Manchester and Liverpool District Banking Co.

STAFFORD is the capital, but by no means the largest town, of Staffordshire, at the termination of the Trent Valley Loop, by which it is 132 miles from London. Population, 12,532. Two members are returned. Boots and shoes are the chief articles of manufacture. Near to a ford on the Sow, Elfleda or Ethelfleda, Alfred's daughter, a great virago who reigned over Mercia, built a castle in the year 913. This was improved by the Normans, but reduced in the civil war; some remains of the keep are yet seen at *Stafford Castle*, a seat of Lord Stafford, 1½ mile to the west.

It is a long straggling town, with short streets branching out of the main thoroughfare (which bear curious names), where the best buildings stand, not far from the two parish churches.

Extract from Bradshaw's Guide 1866 as seen on TV.
(Reprinted by Middleton Press)

14.		During the total rebuild in 1960-62, a spacious new footbridge was provided, plus an unglazed one for parcel and mail traffic. Platform 7 was dedicated to postal traffic and was next to the sorting office. A class 221 Super Voyager electric speeds south on 23rd March 2009 and passes EMU no. 350130 waiting with the 14.04 Liverpool Lime Street to Birmingham New Street. (M.J.Stretton)

15.		The new entrance was enhanced with some red cedar boarding on the generous canopy. The record is from 12th September 2012. (H.Ballantyne)

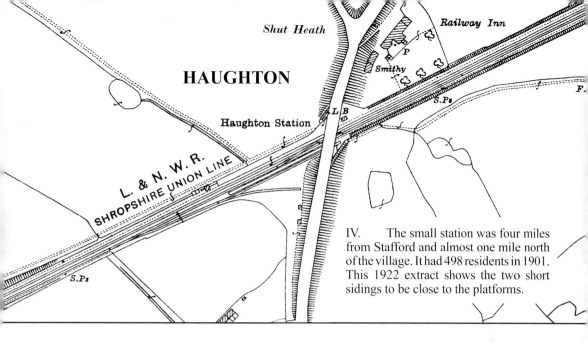

HAUGHTON

Shut Heath

Railway Inn

Smithy

Haughton Station

L. & N. W. R.
SHROPSHIRE UNION LINE

S.Ps

IV.   The small station was four miles from Stafford and almost one mile north of the village. It had 498 residents in 1901. This 1922 extract shows the two short sidings to be close to the platforms.

16.   We are looking towards Stafford in 1949 and can see the platform access on the left, near the fence. The former had been lengthened since the map was produced. The station facilities are under the arch on the left and the next picture is from the foot crossing under the centre arch. (Stations UK)

17.   The box on the right contained a ground frame, which was taken out of use on 22nd June 1958. Passenger service had ceased on 23rd May 1949, but goods continued until 5th August 1957. There were no platform shelters, as you could stand under the bridge, if necessary. (Stations UK)

GNOSALL

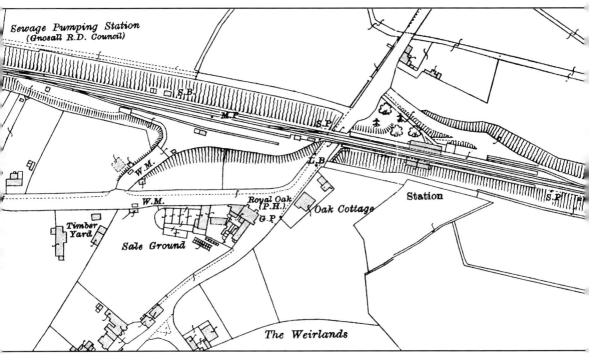

V.   This section of the route is on an embankment and separate inclined roadways serve the goods yard and the up platform. A small cattle market is included on this 1922 map. By 1938, there was a 5-ton goods crane in the yard.

18.   This is the view west and all buildings were of timber construction to minimise the weight on the embankment. The name is usually spoken as "Noss-all", but early timetables showed only one "l". It was first recorded as "Geneshalle", in 1086. (P.Laming coll.)

19.   Some railways made no provision for the comfort of ladies, notably the Shropshire &
Montgomeryshire. Others had small discreet signs; the lamps here are equally modest.
(P.Laming coll.)

20.   This is the only view we have of the station exterior. It also features Gnosall Sports in 1906,
but we can offer no explanation for the presence of an iron bedstead with sanitary items on the
ground. The location is east of Oak Cottage. (P.Laming coll.)

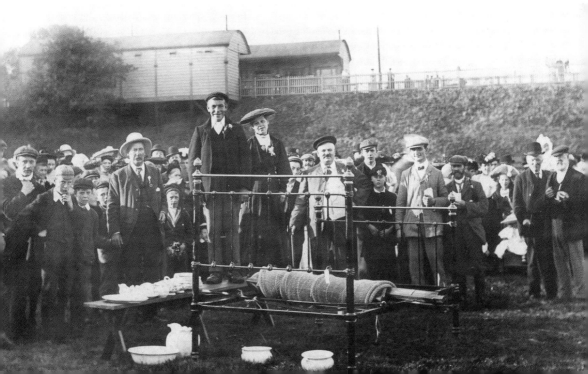

21.　　Although identical in section, the buildings differed in length, the up one (left) being the longer. This 1949 photograph shows them to be in good condition, but deficient in outside seating. (Stations UK)

22.　　Seldom did ex-GWR stock appear on the route but "Hall" class 4-6-0 no. 5962 *Wantage Hall* made a fine sight when diverted via Stafford on its journey to Wolverhampton Low Level from Shrewsbury. This was due to a bridge being built at Shifnal in about 1960. (W.A.Camwell/SLS coll.)

23. Running to Stafford on the same day with a local train is class 4MT 2-6-4T no. 42668. This type was introduced by the LMS in 1934 and was very successful. (W.A.Camwell/SLS coll.)

June 1951

STAFFORD, WELLINGTON AND SHREWSBURY

Miles.		WEEKDAYS													SUNDAYS				
		p. m.	p. m.	a. m.	a. m.	a. m.	noon	p. m.	p. m.	p. m.	p. m.	p. m.	p. m.	p. m.	a. m.	p. m.	p. m.	p. m.	p. m.
—	50**London** (Euston) dep.	9B25	9J25	12 2	.	8 30	12C 0	...	2 30	...	...	5 20	...	...	...	2 50	...	4 55	...
—	50Birmingham (N.S.) ,,	11B10	11J15	5F56	7 10	11 25	1 45	.	3 50	.	4 50	6 24	.	8 20	9 5	5 45	.	6 35	.
		a. m.	a. m.																
0	**Stafford** ....dep.	1 0	2 10	7 22	8 55	12 52	3 42	.	5 35	.	6 22	8 22	.	9 29	10 40	6 50	.	9 30	.
6	Gnosall	...	...	7 32	9 5	1 2	3 52	...	5 45	...	6 32	8 34	...	9 39	10 50	7 0	...	...	...
11½	Newport	.	.	7 41	9 14	1 12	4 1	5 45	5 54	.	6 42	8 47	.	9 49	10 59	7 9	.	.	.
14¾	Donnington	1 29	...	7 49	9 23	1 21	4 9	5 51	6 2	...	6 50	8 55	...	9 55	11 6	7 16	...	9 59	...
16½	Trench Crossing............	1 34	.	7 53	9 27	1 25	4 15	5 55	6 6	.	6 56	8 59	.	9 59	11 10	7 20	.	10 7	.
17½	Hadley **P**	...	...	7 58	9 31	1 30	4 19	5 59	6 10	...	7 0	9 3	...	10 3	11 14	7 24	...	...	...
18¾	**Wellington P** arr.	.	Mondays excepted	8 3	9 36	1 36	4 25	6 4	6 15	.	7 5	9 8	.	10 8	11 19	7 29	.	10 15	.
—	**Wellington P** dep.	Mondays only		8 9	9 42	1 41	4 28	...	...	6 22	7 10	...	9 16	10 13	...	...	8 8	...	10 34
20¼	Admaston ...... Z			8 12	9 45	1 45	4 32	Third Class only.	.	.	7 14	.	9 20	.	.	.	.	.	.
22¾	Walcot .... Z			8 18	9 51	1 51	4 38		...	6 28	7 20	...	9 25	...	...	...	...	...	...
25¼	Upton Magna... Z.....,			8 24	9 57	1 57	4 44		.	.	7 26	.	9SO30	.	.	.	.	.	.
29	**Shrewsbury**... Z ... arr.		3 1	8 32	10 5	2 5	4 52		...	6 38	7 34	...	9 38	10 28	...	...	8 23	...	10 50
	Aberystwyth arr.	.	7W 7	...	2W11	6W 2	9W42		.	.	.	.	.	.	.	.	.	.	.
	Barmouth ... ,,	...	7W57	...	2W36	6W38	9R35		...	...	...	...	...	...	...	...	...	...	...

Miles.		WEEKDAYS													SUNDAYS				
		a. m.	a. m.	a. m.	a. m.	p. m.	a. m.	p. m.	p. m.	p. m.	p. m.	p. m.	p. m.	p. m.	a. m.	a. m.	p. m.	p. m.	p. m.
	Barmouth ...dep.	...	...	...	7R18	...	9W35	12W20	...	...	2W 0	...	...	5W30	...	...	.	...	...
	Aberystwyth ,,	.	.	.	7W10	.	10W 0	12W50	.	.	2W30	.	.	6W 0	.	.	...	.	.
0	**Shrewsbury** Z ... dep.	6 35	...	7 50	11 25	12 20	3 10	4 35	...	5 50	8 10	...	...	11 25	10 3	...	7 35	...	...
3¾	Upton Magna... Z	6 43	.	7 57	11 35	12 26	3 17	.	.	5 56	8 19	.	.	.	.	.	7 43	.	.
6¼	Walcot .... Z	6 48	...	8 1	11 40	12 31	3 22	...	...	6 1	8 24	...	...	...	...	...	7 47	...	...
8¾	Admaston ...... Z	6 53	.	8 5	11 45	12 36	3 27	.	.	6 6	8 29	.	.	.	.	.	.	.	.
10¼	**Wellington P** arr.	6 57	...	8 11	11 50	12 41	3 32	4 55	...	6 11	8 38	...	...	11 40	10 24	...	8 0	...	...
—	**Wellington P** dep.	Stop	7 5	8 14	11 52	12 43	3 38	.	5 20	6 15	.	9 5	10 10	11 45	.	11 40	.	8 14	10 45
11½	Hadley **P**	...	7 10	8 17	11 55	12 47	3 41	...	5 24	6 19	...	9 8	10 14	...	...	11 43	...	8 17	...
12½	Trench Crossing............	.	7 14	8 20	11 58	12 50	3 44	.	5 28	6 22	.	9 11	10 17	.	.	11 46	.	8 20	10 51
14¼	Donnington	a. m.	7 21	8 28	12 4	12 56	3 50	...	5 32	6 28	...	9 18	10 23	...	...	11 50	...	8 24	10 56
17½	Newport	7 0	7 29	8 37	12 11	1 3	3 57	.	5 39	6 36	.	9 25	10 31	.	.	11 57	.	8 31	.
23	Gnosall	7 9	7 39	8 47	12 21	...	4 7	...	Third Class only	6 46	...	9 35	10 41	...	...	12 7	...	8 41	...
29	**Stafford** .... arr.	7 20	7 52	8 58	12 35	1 27	4 23	.		6 57	.	9 46	10 52	12 13	.	12 20	.	8 52	.
57¼	50Birmingham (N.S.)arr.	.	9 16	10 44	2A16	2 54	5 51	.	.	9 4	.	11 25	.	5 30	.	2 10	.	10 11	.
162½	50**London** (Euston) ,,	...	11 17	1 4	3G20	5E45	8D20	...	...	11 6	...	...	...	6 1	...	6 13	...	4 20	...

A—Applies Saturdays only.
B—Sunday night.
C—On Saturdays depart London (Euston) 12.5 p.m.
D—On Fridays arrives London (Euston) 8.35 p.m.
E—On Saturdays arrives London (Euston) 5.17 p.m.
F—On Saturdays until September 8th inclusive departs Birmingham (N. St) 6.20 a.m.
G—On Saturdays arrives London (Euston) 3.27 p.m.
J—Saturdays excepted.
P—For additional trains between Wellington and Hadley, see Table 76.
R—Via Ruabon.
SO—Saturdays only.
W—Via Welshpool.
Z—For additional trains between Wellington and Shrewsbury, see the time table for London (Paddington), Bristol and West of England, South and North Wales, Birmingham, Gloucester, Worcester, West Midlands.

24.   Evident is the signal box, which was closed in 1965. It is seen in 1957, along with the boundary between solid and supported platforms. (Stations UK)

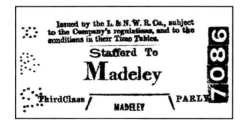

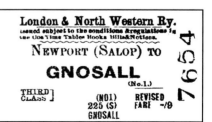

25.   Local passenger service ceased on 7th September 1964 and freight on 1st June of that year. BR class 5 4-6-0 no. 73036 calls on 21st July 1964, bound for Wellington. (D.A.Johnson)

26.   Running through on 27th August 1964 is class 8F 2-8-0 no. 48738 with freight destined for Shrewsbury. The population was 2047 in 1901 and 2482 in 1961. (D.A.Johnson)

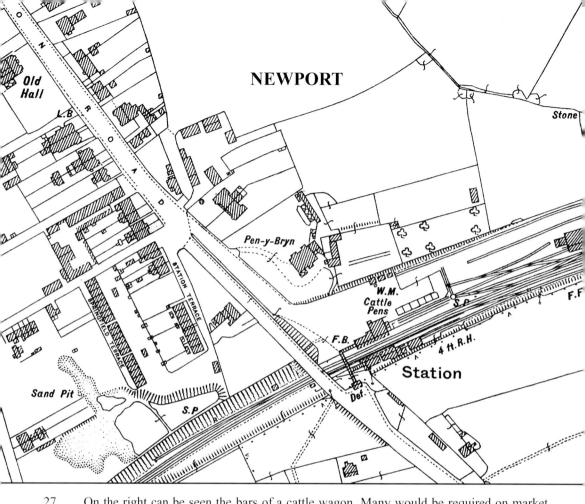

NEWPORT

Old Hall
Pen-y-Bryn
Stone
W.M. Cattle Pens
F.B.
4 ft. R.H.
Station
Def.
S.P.
F.F
Sand Pit
S.P.

27.   On the right can be seen the bars of a cattle wagon. Many would be required on market days. This early postcard may show the crowds on one such day. (P.Laming coll.)

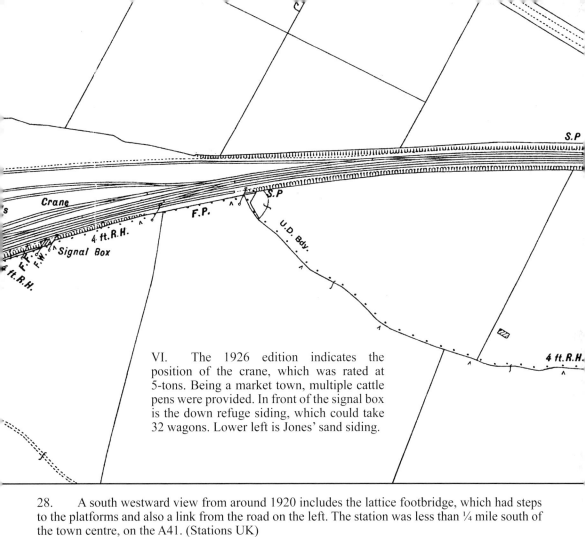

S.P

Crane

's

F.P.

S.P

4 ft. R.H.

U.D. Bdy.

Signal Box

F.W.

F.F.

4 ft. R.H.

4 ft. R.H.

VI.	The 1926 edition indicates the position of the crane, which was rated at 5-tons. Being a market town, multiple cattle pens were provided. In front of the signal box is the down refuge siding, which could take 32 wagons. Lower left is Jones' sand siding.

28.	A south westward view from around 1920 includes the lattice footbridge, which had steps to the platforms and also a link from the road on the left. The station was less than ¼ mile south of the town centre, on the A41. (Stations UK)

29.   Opposite the goods shed, in the mist, is the 1877 signal box, which had 28 levers and closed on 22nd November 1969. This 1949 record includes a small canopy on the down side, which probably predates the others. (Stations UK)

NEWPORT.

POPULATION, 2,856.

A telegraph station.

HOTELS. — Royal Victoria, Crown.

MARKET DAY.—Saturday.   FAIRS.—1st Tuesday in February, Saturday before Palm Sunday, May 28th, July 27th, September 25th, and December 10th.

BANKERS.—National Provincial Bank of England

Here is a fine church of the 15th century, and in the vicinity are *Chetwynd Park* and *Aqualate Hall* and *Mere*, a fine sheet of water covering nearly 200 acres.

Extract from Bradshaw's Guide 1866 as seen on TV. (Reprinted by Middleton Press)

30.   A stopping train enters the up platform, where the facilities for gentlemen are seen to be roofless. The main roof is impressive, with its massive blue pantiles. They are seen in about 1960. (D.Lawrence)

31.   BR class 5 4-6-0 no. 73090 has just passed over the staff crossing as it comes in with a stopping train from Shrewsbury, in about 1963. The population grew from 3241 in 1901 to 4920 in 1961. (D.Wilson)

32. The 5.59pm to Wellington is departing on 27th August 1964, behind class 4 2-6-4T no. 42400. This design was introduced by the LMS in 1927. The line from Stafford was closed on 1st August 1966. (D.Johnson)

33. Arriving on 29th August 1964 is no. 73025, a BR class 5 4-6-0. Above the leading coach can be seen part of the massive grain silo built by the Ministry of Food just prior to World War II. A siding was extended to it from the goods yard. This closed on 1st July 1968, four years after passenger services had ceased. (D.Wilson)

DONNINGTON

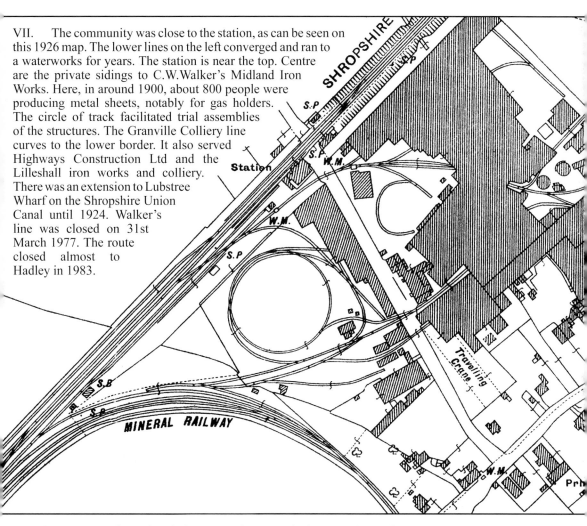

VII.   The community was close to the station, as can be seen on this 1926 map. The lower lines on the left converged and ran to a waterworks for years. The station is near the top. Centre are the private sidings to C.W. Walker's Midland Iron Works. Here, in around 1900, about 800 people were producing metal sheets, notably for gas holders. The circle of track facilitated trial assemblies of the structures. The Granville Colliery line curves to the lower border. It also served Highways Construction Ltd and the Lilleshall iron works and colliery. There was an extension to Lubstree Wharf on the Shropshire Union Canal until 1924. Walker's line was closed on 31st March 1977. The route closed almost to Hadley in 1983.

34.   Our earliest view is from a card postmarked 1907. The staff seem to have brought their children for a cheap photograph. The small building on the right is the parcels shed. (P. Laming coll.)

35. The fenestrated chimneys, the stone quoins and the up waiting room show more clearly on this postcard. The signal box is No. 1. (P.Laming coll.)

36. Blowing off is an ex-LMS class 5 4-6-0 no. 44835, as it leaves for Wellington in about 1950. Both public goods facilities and passenger services were withdrawn on 7th September 1964. (W.A.Camwell/SLS)

37.   The iron works shows in all four photographs and the crossing and box are clearest in this 1954 view. The latter is Donnington No. 1; it had 24 levers and was in use from 1881 until 1969. No. 2 had 32 and served in the same period and is lower left on the map. (Stations UK)

SOUTH OF DONNINGTON

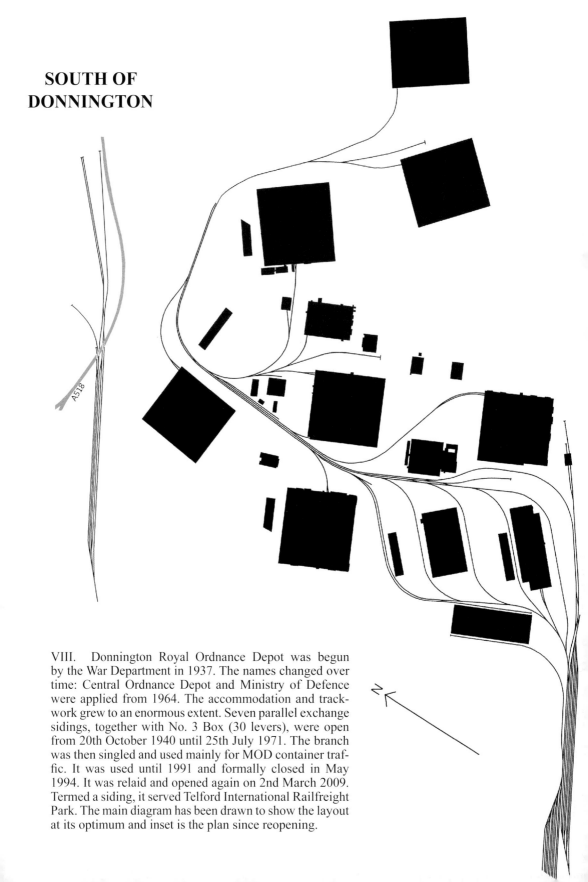

VIII. Donnington Royal Ordnance Depot was begun by the War Department in 1937. The names changed over time: Central Ordnance Depot and Ministry of Defence were applied from 1964. The accommodation and track-work grew to an enormous extent. Seven parallel exchange sidings, together with No. 3 Box (30 levers), were open from 20th October 1940 until 25th July 1971. The branch was then singled and used mainly for MOD container traffic. It was used until 1991 and formally closed in May 1994. It was relaid and opened again on 2nd March 2009. Termed a siding, it served Telford International Railfreight Park. The main diagram has been drawn to show the layout at its optimum and inset is the plan since reopening.

38. A small part of the massive MOD depot is seen in about 1990, with a Ruston Hornsby diesel 0-6-0 hauling two flat wagons. They had probably carried containers from Bicester or Marchwood MOD depots. (A.Dudman coll.)

39. No. 47238 has just arrived with a single van from Shrewsbury Coton Hill on 6th July 1990. The terminal was a commercial failure and was soon taken out of use, although not officially closed. It reopened as stated. (P.D.Shannon)

40.   No. 66143 waits on 17th December 2009 while military containers are unloaded. Running on Thursdays only, the train had come from Warrington's Arpley Yard. (P.D.Shannon)

41.   It is 14th July 2011 and no. 66070 has just arrived with more containers for the depot. This panorama is southwest from the road bridge. Stored on the right are class 508 EMUs and a line of Network Rail infrastructure wagons. (P.D.Shannon)

TRENCH CROSSING

IX.   The village of Trench can be seen to be nearby on this map of 1926, the Post Office being shown on the main road. There were no goods sidings.

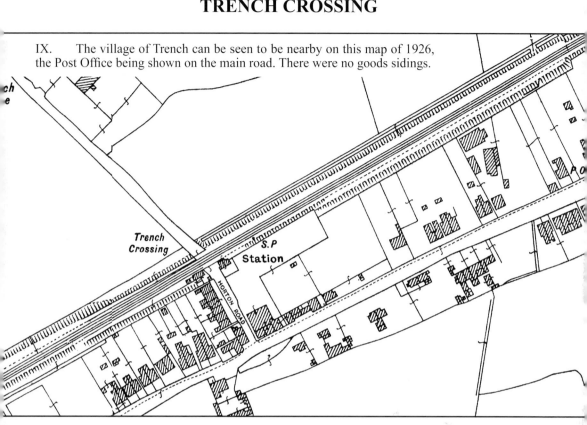

42.   This station opened after the others, on 1st January 1855, and so the crossing was there before the station needed a name. There was generous provision for ladies, but no roof for gentlemen, next door. (Lens of Sutton)

43.   The same structures are seen from the north side of the level crossing, which was timber decked. Loose road stone for horses to disperse was not ideal; tarmac was not yet available. (P.Laming coll.)

44.   The crossing was controlled by a ground frame and the gates were the original type of iron ones. The staff accommodation is now in view. The crossing keeper would usually occupy the nearest part. This is a 1954 record. (Stations UK)

45.   The up side is seen to be particularly featureless, as BR class 5 no. 73025 arrives in about 1958. The name boards are fixed to the seats to minimise expense on posts. (A.J.B.Dodd)

46.   "Jubilee" class 4-6-0 no. 45577 *Bengal* arrives on 21st July 1964. It will depart at 4.31pm for Shrewsbury. The term HALT was not shown, although some BR tickets carried it. (D.A.Johnson)

WEST OF
TRENCH CROSSING

X.   Our journey is from right to left and the signal box on the left was called Trench Sidings. It opened in June 1881 and closed in April 1968. Note that the canal runs close to the 1866 Wombridge Branch, on this 1927 edition. At the end of the line, there was a siding to Russell's Rubber Works. The private sidings closed in 1946.

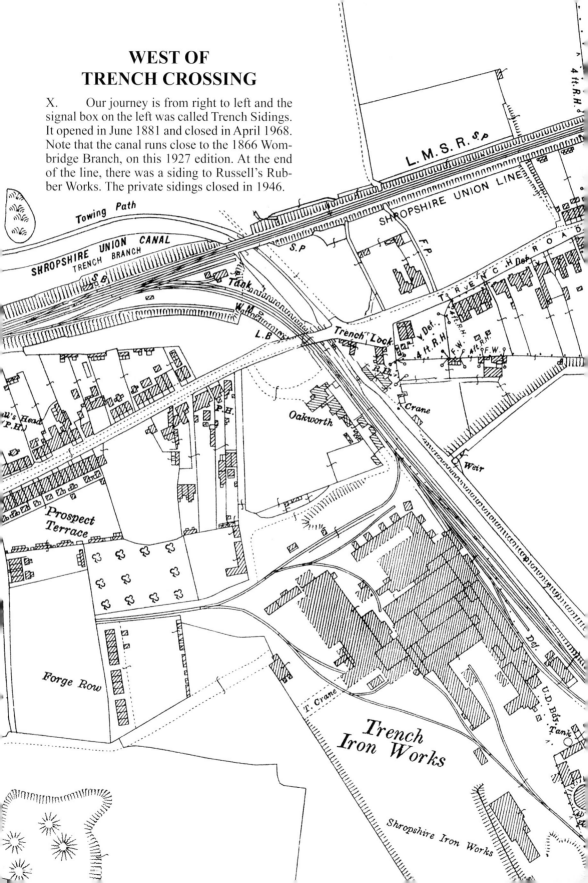

47. This small engine shed opened in around 1870 and is shown in the branch junction, near the word Tank on map X. The depot was in use until 1943 and was photographed in 1959. 0-4-0STs nos 16004 and 16027 were regular residents here and were based at Shrewsbury. (R.S.Carpenter)

XI.   Our route is across this 1937 edition and curving from Hadley Junction is the branch to Coalport, shown herein from picture 70 onwards. There is a small gap between the right of this map and the left of the previous one. Castle Works was owned by Nettlefold & Chamberlain in 1870, but closed in 1886. It reopened in June 1900 until May 1904 and was used for the manufacture of tramcars by G.F.Milnes & Co. Ltd. In 1905-08, it was used by the Metropolitan Amalgamated Railway Carriage & Wagon Co. Ltd. It was taken over for the production of domestic sanitary items and vehicle parts by J.Sankey & Sons Ltd. from 1911. The siding were closed in 1972 and removed in 1984.

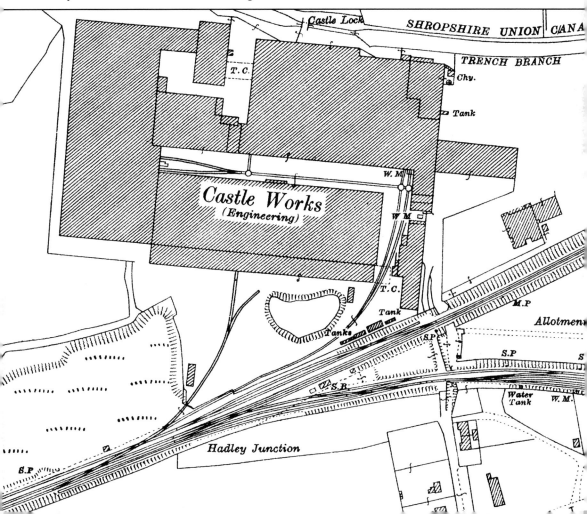

48.   Hadley Junction exchange sidings are featured in this view from April 1949. They are on the right of map XI. Passing with a train from Coalport is class 3 2-6-2T no. 40048, while ex-LNWR "Coal Engine" no. 28152 waits in the sidings. (M.Whitehouse)

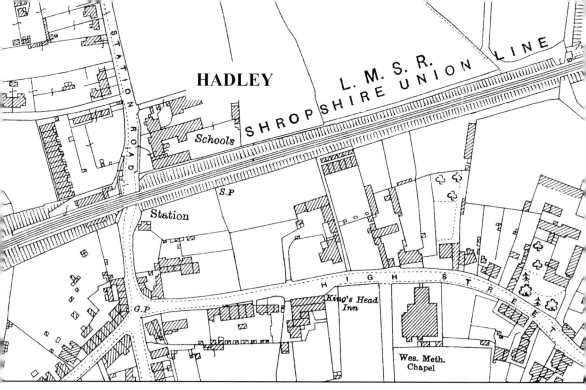

HADLEY

L. M. S. R. LINE

SHROPSHIRE UNION

Schools

S.P

Station

G.P

King's Head Inn

HIGH STREET

Wes. Meth. Chapel

XII. The 1927 survey indicates the proximity of the High Street to the station. Prominent is the Wesleyan Methodist Chapel. The population grew from 3160 in 1901 to 5088 in 1961.

49. Money was lavished on expensive and stylish barge boards in preference to simple weather protection. At least the steps down to Station Road (right) are covered. This and the next view are from 1954. (Stations UK)

50. Access to the down platform (right) was by way of the boarded crossing in the distance. The station had a greatly improved service after the Coalport branch opened in 1861 and a depleted one on its closure in 1952. (Stations UK)

EAST OF WELLINGTON

51.　　This is Stafford Junction on 9th August 1932, although the 22-lever box was called Wellington No. 1. It is two miles from the station. The Stafford lines are on the left and the Wolverhampton ones on the right. The former had a siding on the south side serving Haybridge Steel Works until 16th May 1964. (Mowat coll.)

52.　　Seen in about 1958 is ex-GWR motive power leaving what was ex-GWR track. The diagram on the back cover explains this. The box was in use from its completion in about 1880 until 10th September 1967. The southern track to Donnington was taken out of use on 25th July 1971. The loco shown is no. 6903 *Belmont Hall*. (A.J.B.Dodd)

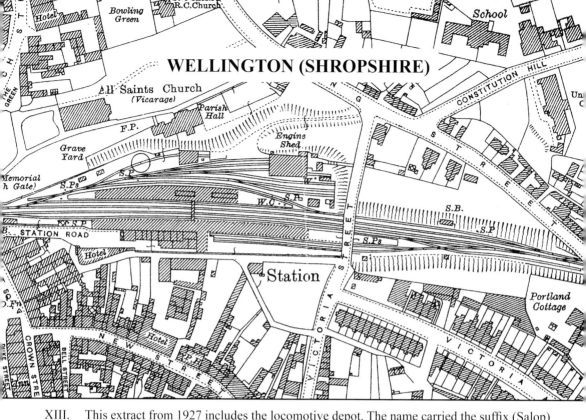

WELLINGTON (SHROPSHIRE)

XIII.   This extract from 1927 includes the locomotive depot. The name carried the suffix (Salop) in the early BR years and "for Telford" from 16th May 1983. This was changed to "Telford West" on 12th May 1986, to reduce confusion, and dropped on 28th May 1994. The first goods shed also housed locomotives.

53.   There were initially two short staggered platforms, linked by a wooden foot crossing. The goods yard and goods shed were north of them, but this area was eventually used for the locomotive depot. This is the earliest platform view that we have. (Lens of Sutton coll.)

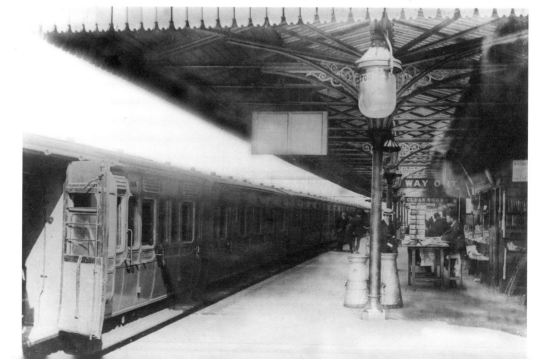

54.   Two bay platforms were created on the south side in the 1860s, after the Coalport branch opened. One such train is seen in the 1930s, standing behind class 3F 0-6-2T no. 7734. The coaches are six-wheelers. (R.S.Carpenter coll.)

55.   The up platform became an island in about 1880 and the same locomotive is departing from it in 1935, with a stopping train to Stafford. Included is No. 2 Box, which was in use between about 1880 and 1953. Its successor had 71 levers and remained in use until 19th November 2012. Nos 3 and 4 were west of the station. (R.S.Carpenter coll.)

56.   A Coalport branch train waits to leave platform 6, the southern bay, on 3rd August 1935, behind "Cauliflower" class 0-6-0 no. 8583. The LMS had operated slip coaches here on trains from London via Stafford and some via Wolverhampton. (H.F.Wheeller/R.S.Carpenter coll.)

57.   Seen on the same day is a train bound for Stafford behind "Patriot" class 4-6-0 no. 5508. Leading is a horse box and next is a ventilated van for perishable foodstuffs. (H.F.Wheeller/R.S.Carpenter coll.)

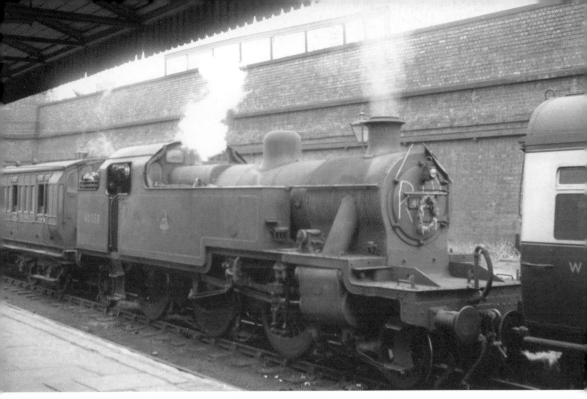

58.　　Ex-LMS 2-6-2T no. 40058 has worked the 2.35pm from Coalport on 31st May 1952, the last day of passenger service on the branch. Under the wreath is chalked R.I.P. Platform 6 died on 8th March 1969. (T.G.Wassell/H.Davies coll.)

59.　　Waiting to depart for Shrewsbury on 28th June 1965 is a Western Region locomotive with a London Midland Region coach. The former is no. 7915 *Mere Hall*. (G.Adams/M.J.Stretton coll.)

60.   The 12.20 to Stafford on 18th April 1959 was hauled by class 4P 2-6-4T no. 42400, one of a batch with side windows introduced by the LMS in 1933. Above its dome is the roof of the coal stage. (D.A.Johnson)

61.   The depot was photographed on 24th August 1960, with the asbestos clad coaling area on the left. The three-road shed was created from the original goods shed in 1867, only the right line running though the wall at the other end. Closure came on 10th August 1964. (R.G.Nelson/T.Walsh coll.)

62.   Looking east in 1956 we see SALOP stated boldly. This was necessary until 1964, when the station with the same name, between Taunton and Exeter, closed. The pointed roof can be seen more fully in picture 63. The suffix was reapplied with effect from the 29th September 1996, but this time in full - SHROPSHIRE. (Stations UK)

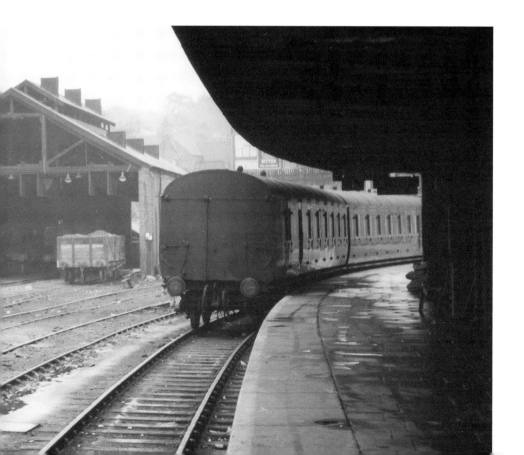

63.   This is the station approach along Station Road in April 1983. Platform 1 (nearest) could take seven coaches, No. 2 ten and No. 3 four. (D.A.Thompson)

64.	"Grange" class 4-6-0 no. 6829 *Burmington Grange* accelerates the 5.10pm Shrewsbury to Wolverhampton Low Level on 21st July 1962. This class was introduced in 1936. (L.W.Rowe)

65.	The two centre roads were often used for freight as the majority of passenger services stopped here in later years. Ex-GWR "Pannier" 0-6-0PT no. 3754 creeps through on 3rd July 1964, with its rattling train of loose coupled wagons. (J.M.Tolson/F.Hornby)

66. Arriving on 24th June 1989 is no. 47613 *North Star* with the 09.40 Euston to Aberystwyth. Such through trains would soon come to be discontinued. (T.Heavyside)

67.　　The 11.33 Shrewsbury to Birmingham New Street was recorded on 24th June 1989. It is at platform No. 1 and the stops of No. 3 are visible lower left. (T.Heavyside)

Other views can be seen in the *Craven Arms to Wellington* and *Wolverhampton to Shrewsbury* albums from Middleton Press.

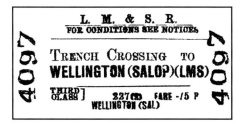

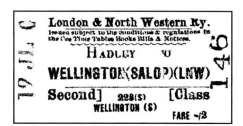

68.   Waiting at platform No. 2 is no. 170506, bound for Shrewsbury on 6th August 2008. Most of the structures date from around 1880. (M.J.Stretton)

69.   We look at the former island platform from a train bound for Wrexham on 26th June 2008. From 16th December 2002, the all-electric signalling was controlled from Madeley Junction. However, the West Midlands Signalling Centre at Saltley took over on 19th November 2012. (V.Mitchell)

Coalport Branch

IV.   The branch runs from top left on this 1938 edition at 6ins to a mile. Oakengates station is a little above centre. Close to the corner is Wombridge Ballast Tip Siding, which was added in 1912 and removed in about 1940. Above it is evidence of the line which served Wombridge Iron Works from 1873 until 1932. The GWR main line is shown on the left, together with its Oakengates (West) station. The remainder of its route is not clear as it is partly in Oakengates Tunnel, which is 471 yards long. It is here that the Coalport branch runs over it near its summit level - see the gradient profile in the introduction. The mineral railway shown top right connects with the LMS branch and served Granville Colliery, Grange Colliery, Newyard Works (shown) and Snedshill Iron Works. The siding to Priors Lee Steel Works and furnaces diverges above the tunnel and continues to an asphalt works and various tips. Off the map it ran to Woodhouse Colliery, Lawn Colliery, Stafford Colliery and Park Lane Colliery. The coal and iron mines, plus the furnaces in this area were mostly owned by the Lilleshall Company, as were the railways serving them.

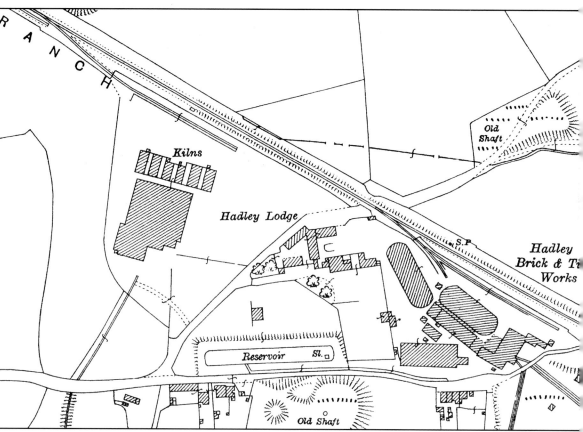

XV.   We saw the commencement of the branch at the exchange sidings in picture no. 48. Here are the first two private sidings on the route. The 1927 map shows both of Blockley's sidings. The one on the right came in 1897 and the other in 1926. Map II shows the entire branch and is a good guide to the remainder of the journey.

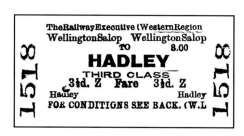

→ XVI. The following is an enlargement of the central part of the map XIV, but is from 1927. Market Street station is at the top and West station is on the left. The latter can be seen in our *Wolverhampton to Shrewsbury* album. The route on the right is the one from the top right of map XIV and is shown here to have a siding to Snedshill Iron Works. An unusual feature of the Saw Mill was that it was a business with private sidings from competing railway companies. The main lines were at similar levels near the centre of the map, where the branch climbed at 1 in 50 over the GWR's tunnel. The mineral railway was part of the Lilleshall empire.

OAKENGATES
MARKET STREET

Cinema

STATION HILL

Station · S.B.

Police
Station

Prim.
Meth.
Chapel

P.H. · *Hall*

Def.

OXFORD STREET

MARKET STREET

*Fighting
Cocks*
(P.H.)

Bk

Goods Shed

S.P.

*Caledonian
Hotel*

P.H.

Saw Mill

Goods
Shed
Cr

W.M.

Station

F.B.

F.B. · F.P.

*Iron
Foundry*

S.P.

S.P.

S.P.

Sluice

SHREWSBURY & BIRMINGHAM

G. W. R.

STATION ROAD

S.P.

MINERAL RAILWAY

Reservoir

Snedsh

Chy.

70.　The suffix was not added until 18th June 1951, less than a year before closure to passengers on the branch. This eastward view had the level crossing on the left and the station entrance on the right. (P.Laming coll.)

71.　We are looking west over the station with the crossing and the cinema on the right. The latter is mentioned on the last map. (Lens of Sutton coll.)

72.   A northward panorama from July 1932 has the partially disused goods yard on the left.
The tall building on the right is shown as "Prim. Meth." meaning Primitive Methodist. They were
"Prim and Proper", with strict constraints, but merged in about 1930 with mainstream Methodism.
(Mowat coll./R.S.Carpenter coll.)

73.   An August 1932 view reveals that the down platform was out of use by that time and that
it once had a spacious building, probably for parcels. (R.S.Carpenter coll.)

74.   We look north in 1952 and see the open doorway to the waiting area and the discreet sign for the benefit of gentlemen. (Stations UK)

75.   A sequence of views from the late 1950s from one local photographer can now be enjoyed. With the snow, the yard looks very spacious. There were two sidings on the right, used by the Co-op until 2nd March 1958. (A.J.B.Dodd)

76. The difference in level between the yard and the running lines is evident in this and the next view. Brake vans often accompanied engines on their return journey to maintain stock balance. (A.J.B.Dodd)

77. Ex-GWR engines, such as this 0-6-0PT, appeared after the regional boundary changes. The chimney on the left is on the goods office. (A.J.B.Dodd)

78.   The 1890 box only worked the points north of the crossing, the others being by key-interlocked ground frames. (A.J.B.Dodd)

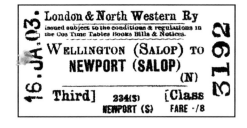

16.JA.03.

London & North Western Ry

issued subject to the conditions & regulations in the Cos Time Tables Books Bills & Notices.

WELLINGTON (SALOP) TO

NEWPORT (SALOP)

(N)

Third]   234(S)   [Class

NEWPORT (S)   FARE -/8

3192

L M & S R
FOR CONDITIONS
SEE BACK
Available 1 Cal.Month
PRIVILEGE TICKET
THIRD CLASS

Coalport
TO
WELLINGTON (SALOP)
Via Hadley
234 (PTR)
COALPORT

L. M. & S. R.

Available for 7 Days
PRIVILEGE TICKET

THIRD CLASS

Wellington (Salop)
TO
COALPORT (LMS)
Via Hadley

Fare -/7½

789   789

79.   The loop was taken out of use on 2nd March 1958, as were the two sidings for the Co-op and the private one to the shed of B & A Millington, seen on the left of picture 72. The remaining running line is undergoing repairs. (A.J.B.Dodd)

80.   This sad view was recorded at about the time of the closure of the northern part of the route on 6th July 1964. The yard here closed that day. The gates were hand operated. Note the relics and tips on the skyline. (Lens of Sutton coll.)

SOUTH OF OAKENGATES

81.   Only Granville Colliery remained open to be nationalised in 1947. The last train left it on 2nd October 1979. Most ran to power stations, via Donnington. Priors Lee exchange sidings are seen from the 2.35pm Coalport to Wellington on 31st May 1952.
(T.G.Wassell/H.Davies coll.)

82.   Priors Lee sidings had two ground frames like this, one at each end of the exchange sidings. The private sidings serving Priors Lee Steelworks lasted from November 1890 to December 1959. Chalked on the left wall is "The Happy Haven".
(A.J.B.Dodd)

83.   The industrial sites of the Lilleshall businesses were served by the 26 miles of their railway network. Their engine shed was at the New Yard Engineering Works, where the wagon fleet was maintained. There were around 450 at the peak of their network. (A.J.B.Dodd)

84.   Here we look towards Oakengates at the northern end of the exchange sidings. The loading gauge is almost in line with No. 1 Ground Frame. (A.J.B.Dodd)

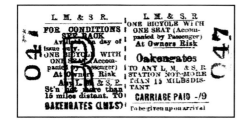

85.   The panorama is between the two main roads shown on the first Oakengates map (no. XIV) and includes ex-LMS class 5 4-6-0 no. 45143, which was based at Shrewsbury. The link to Snedshill sidings is on the right. (A.J.B.Dodd)

86.   Peckett no. 883 of 1901 runs over the peaceful A5, while on a journey across the Lilleshall estate. Their railway system closed in 1958, the pictures being just prior to that time. (A.J.B.Dodd)

87.   A close up of the same locomotive was obtained outside the Lilleshall New Works shed, known as St. Georges. Cameras were seldom carried above plus-fours. (A.J.B.Dodd)

88.　　　Andrew Barclay no. 1496 of 1916 hauls a load of coal from the Granville Colliery exchange sidings towards the Lilleshall system. This company had been formed in 1764 and used that name from 1862-2000. (A.J.B.Dodd)

89.　　　Coupled to Peckett no. 883 of 1901 is the 1913 Andrew Barclay no. 1349 *Alberta* and they are running back to St. Georges, through the woods of the Nabb. Monthly figures in 1870 were coal - 86,000 tons and ironstone - 10,000 tons. By 1890, the steel tonnage was 2800 per month. (A.J.B.Dodd)

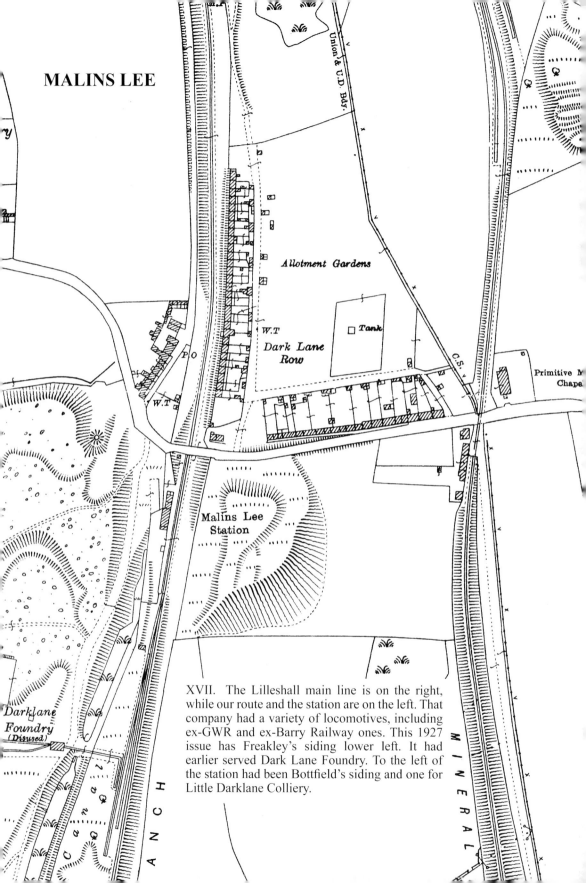

MALINS LEE

Union & U.D. Bdy.

Allotment Gardens

W.T

Dark Lane
Row

☐ Tank

P.O

C.S.

W.T

Primitive M
Chapel

Malins Lee
Station

*Darklane
Foundry*
(Disused)

C A N C H

M I N E R A L

XVII. The Lilleshall main line is on the right,
while our route and the station are on the left. That
company had a variety of locomotives, including
ex-GWR and ex-Barry Railway ones. This 1927
issue has Freakley's siding lower left. It had
earlier served Dark Lane Foundry. To the left of
the station had been Bottfield's siding and one for
Little Darklane Colliery.

90. This and the next station were on the 2½ mile long summit level. As was common practice, fire buckets adorn one wall of the roofless gents.
(R.S.Carpenter coll.)

91. The signalling instruments were in the building, but the levers were on the platform; they are not visible in the pictures. Gardening was clearly an important part of duties.
(Lens of Sutton coll.)

92. The station opened after the others on the branch, on 7th July 1862. It closed briefly between March 1918 and February 1919. The fire buckets have gone and so have the lamps. The north elevation is seen after loss of passenger service in 1952.
(A.J.B.Dodd)

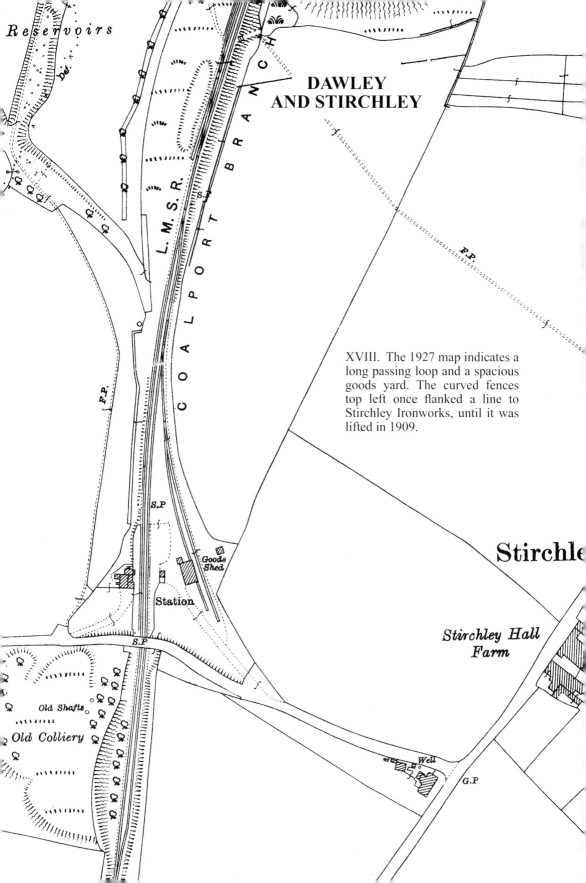

Reservoirs

**DAWLEY
AND STIRCHLEY**

L.M.S.R.

COALPORT BRANCH

S.P.

F.P.

F.P.

XVIII. The 1927 map indicates a
long passing loop and a spacious
goods yard. The curved fences
top left once flanked a line to
Stirchley Ironworks, until it was
lifted in 1909.

Stirchle

S.P.

Goods
Shed

Station

S.P.

Stirchley Hall
Farm

S.P.

Old Shafts

Old Colliery

Well

G.P.

93.   A view north on 9th August 1932 shows DAWLEY AND on a separate board. The reason was that these words were not added to STIRCHLEY until 1st July 1923. (R.S.Carpenter)

94.   There is evidence of a building having been on the down side. Plans show it in the late 19th century. The levers are clearer, as they had white handles by 1950. They were moved from the north end of the platform to near the gate in 1924. (Stations UK)

95. A "Pannier" tank leaves the goods yard to join the down loop, in about 1958. The goods service ceased here on 6th July 1964. (A.J.B.Dodd)

96. The SLS Railtour on 12th September 1959 operated from Stourbridge Junction via Much Wenlock, Longville, Coalport East, Shrewsbury Abbey Foregate Loop, Minsterley, Coleham, Buildwas, Bewdley and Kidderminster. (A.J.B.Dodd)

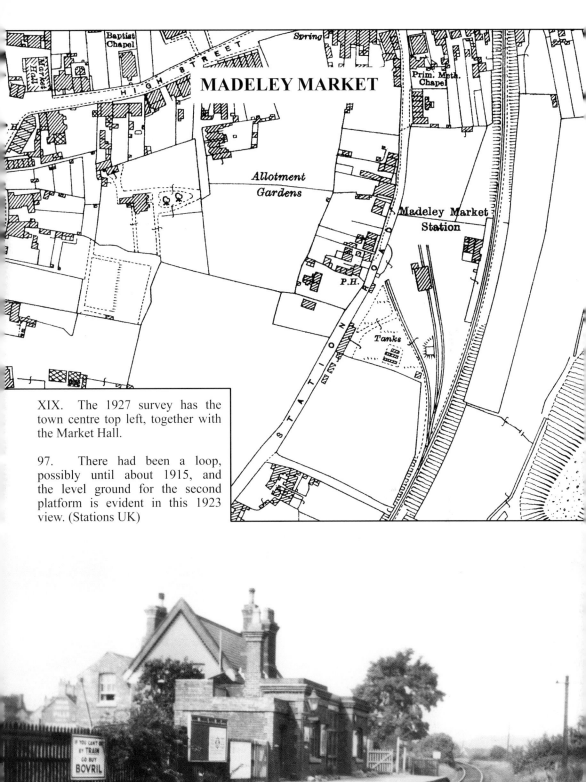

MADELEY MARKET

XIX. The 1927 survey has the town centre top left, together with the Market Hall.

97. There had been a loop, possibly until about 1915, and the level ground for the second platform is evident in this 1923 view. (Stations UK)

98.   The view towards Coalport in 1932 includes three of Sugg's Windsor pattern gas lamps. Built of copper they were still being made in 2014. The station design was similar to its neighbours. (R.S.Carpenter coll.)

99.   LMS class 2F 0-6-2T no. 7836 had climbed gradients as steep as 1 in 31 from Coalport, on 13th August 1947. The train was known locally as the "Coalport Dodger". (SLS coll.)

100.   The drying of clothes in the Black Country had often been problematical, but the Clean Air Act had been passed in 1955, just before this common Monday custom was recorded. This is the only evidence we have that the station was still occupied. (A.J.B.Dodd)

101.   Goods service was withdrawn here and at the terminus on 5th December 1960. The end is nigh, but the important sign remained. (A.J.B.Dodd)

BLISTS HILL

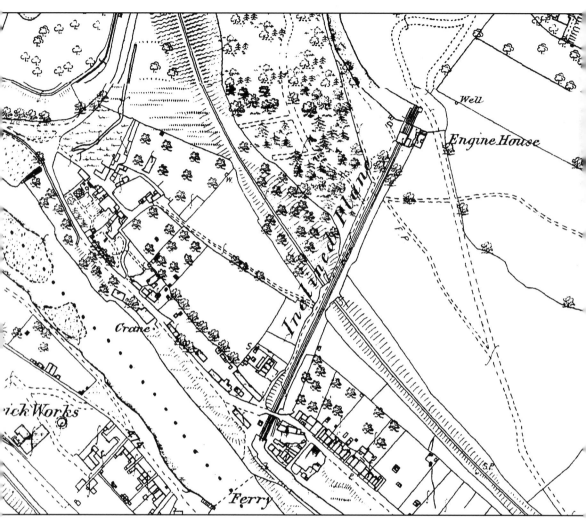

XX.   Our route curves across this map from the 1870s and shows it passing under an extremely unusual railway. It carried only small canal barges, known as tub boats, using two trolleys connected by a rope, through the engine house. The GWR is in the lower left corner and the ferry is across the River Severn.

102.   This is the top of the Hay Inclined Plane, but the vertically bent rails and the winding equipment are absent. The lift was built in 1792-93 to connect the Shropshire Canal with the River Severn and it conveyed coal downhill, the empty tub boats being hauled up with no power needed. The beam engine was used only to pull the load over the cill seen. A 5-ton tub-boat went over 300 yards in 3½ minutes. Closure came in 1907, but the site was soon cleared after the formation of the Ironbridge Gorge Museum Trust in 1968 and rails were laid in 1975-76, although inevitably not of the original pattern. (IGM)

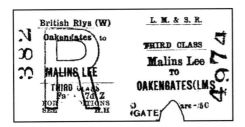
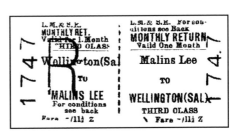

103.   Blists Hill Ironworks had once had a complex tramway system and one line passed over the 1859 Lee Dingle bridge to reach Meadow Pit Colliery, by way of an inclined plane. The works closed in 1912, but the bridge was still standing, albeit devoid of decking, in the 1950s and is seen from a train climbing from Coalport. It was still in place in 2014. At 1 in 31, it was probably the steepest line for standard gauge passenger trains in the UK. (A.J.B.Dodd)

104.   Near the museum's Blists Hill Victorian Town is the former brick and tile works, and running near to it on 28th May 2007 was a replica of Trevithick's 1802 locomotive built by the Coalbrookdale Company. It is doubtful that they finished the original due to a fatality. The one seen was constructed by G.K.N.Sankey. The museum had four other locomotives in its collection. (P.G.Barnes)

105.   With a colliery in the background, the engine takes water, while its chimney cowl is still on. An earlier non-working replica can be seen in Telford in picture 86 in the *Wolverhampton to Shrewsbury* album, but it was lost to public view. The rails would have originally been short cast iron lengths. (P.G.Barnes)

COALPORT EAST

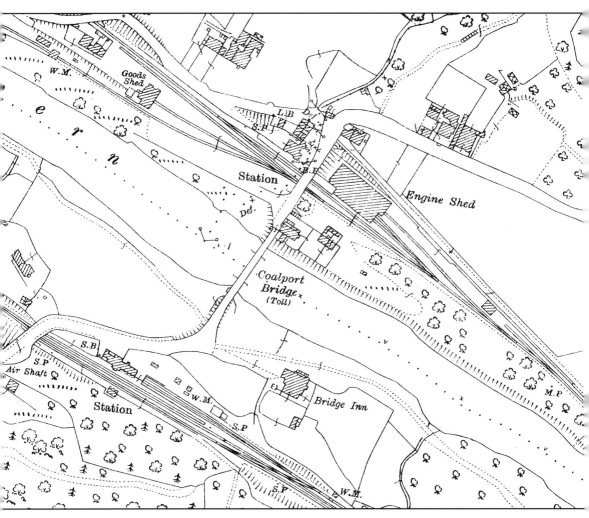

XXI.   The 1927 survey does not present the roadways clearly on the approach to the station, but the next photograph shows the steep gradients. Lower left is the GWR station, which is illustrated in our *Kidderminster to Shrewsbury* album. The suffix EAST came in 1951, but did not appear in timetables.

London & North Western Ry.
Issued subject to the conditions & regulations in the Cos Time Tables Books Bills & Notices.
STIRCHLEY   TO
WELLINGTON(SALOP)(LNW)
VIA HADLEY
Third]   231(S)   [Class
WELLINGTON (S)
TURN OVER)   FARE -/5½

L.M.&S.R.
MONTHLY RETURN
Valid One Month
THIRD CLASS
Oakengates
TO
DAWLEY & S.
For conditions see back
Fare -/5½ Z

L.M.&S.R.   For conditions see back
MONTHLY RETURN
Valid One Month
Dawley & S.
TO
OAKENGATES(LMS
THIRD CLASS
Fare -/5½ Z

106. The station and the bridge over the tracks are on the right. The camera is on the sharp bend on the steep station approach, signed ROAD NOT PUBLIC. The road to the bridge drops between the houses on the left in this postcard view, probably pre-1900. (Lens of Sutton coll.)

107. The southwest elevation is seen from the entrance to the goods yard, as the sun is low. Set low in the hills, the station was unusual in having low shrubs. The oil lamp would have given a low light, although low on the wall. (Lens of Sutton coll.)

108.   A 1932 panorama from the road bridge includes part of the goods yard and ash left by locomotives waiting to depart. Half a mile in the distance was the private siding for the Coalport China Company, but the dates are not available. (R.S.Carpenter coll.)

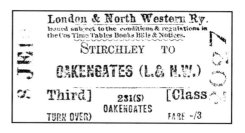

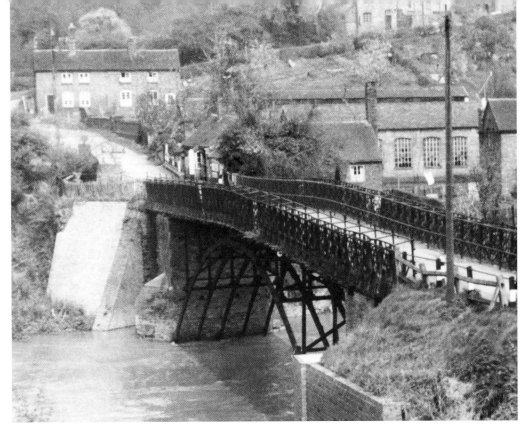

109.   We look north across the toll bridge towards the station in 1959, but only three windows of the carriage shed are visible, on the right. This 1818 bridge is downstream of the famous one and contains iron castings from the previous one here. (H.C.Casserley)

110.   It is 30th July 1932 and there is evidence that it was probably a Monday. We can survey more of the goods yard and also two domestic toilets of the day; known as the privy, they were remote from the home. (R.S.Carpenter)

111. A fine record from 31st October 1935 features 0-6-2T no. 7768 with six-wheeled coaches, often then found in retirement on branch lines. The brake van shows evidence of steam heating in use. The locomotive appears again in the next picture. (W.A.Camwell/SLS)

BRITISH RLYS (W)   BRITISH RLYS (W)
Madeley Market   Madeley Market
TO
COALPORT or
DAWLEY & STIRCHLEY
THIRD CLASS
5½d Z   Fare   5½d Z
FOR CONDITIONS   FOR CONDITIONS
SEE BACK   SEE BACK C-L
6030   6030

L.M.&S.R. For   L.M.&S.R. For
conditions see Back   conditions see Back
THIRD CLASS   THIRD CLASS
SINGLE   SINGLE
Madeley M'ket   Madeley M'ket
Madeley Market   To
HADLEY
Hadley   Hadley
1/4½ Z   FARE   1/4½ Z
2814   2814

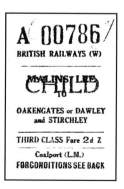

A 00786
BRITISH RAILWAYS (W)

MADELEY LEE
CHILD
TO

OAKENGATES or DAWLEY
and STIRCHLEY

THIRD CLASS Fare 2d Z

Coalport (L.M.)
FOR CONDITIONS SEE BACK

112. The three-track shed was reduced to one operationally for locomotives in 1924. It was a sub-shed to Shrewsbury, which was coded 84G, and closure came on 31st May 1952. The two roads in the shed beyond the left border were once used for coaches. (W.A.Camwell/SLS)

113. We are at the end of the branch in 1939 and witness oiling in progress and the most basic method of coaling. However, such branch-end facilities were usually used only for "topping-up". (R.S.Carpenter coll.)

114.   The ground frame can be seen on the left on 26th April 1947, as ex-LNWR class 2F no. 7755 blows off, prior to leaving at 7.30pm. A full head of steam would have always been the aim before leaving here. (SLS coll.)

115.   Maximum steam production was required for the 1 in 40 climb ahead and so the fireman of no. 28583 is firing earnestly. It is August 1947 and both signals are evident. (M.Whitehouse coll.)

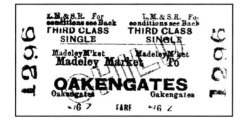

116.   The end of the branch is in the distance and flowers adorn the platform as "Cauliflower" class 0-6-0 no. 28583 waits to depart in August 1947. More ash has been abandoned on the track in the absence of an ashpit. (M.Whitehouse coll.)

117.   We move to September 1947 and the fireman has made as much steam as possible. Of interest in this view is the 1870 lever frame, in the open on the platform. The LMS would exist for only three more months. (M.Whitehouse coll.)

118.   By 1952, only the BR logo and number were kept clean and the train was half the usual length. The end for passengers came that year. Goods traffic continued until 5th December 1960. (P.Kingston)

119.   "The Shropshire Rail Tour" called on 23rd April 1955, hauled by "Dean Goods" 0-6-0 no. 2516, with GWR on its tender. There were then no limits for photographers. (M.Whitehouse coll.)

120.   The final tour was on 12th September 1959 and its extent is mentioned in caption 96.
Serious students on the left examine the lever frame, the rodding tunnel for which is evident to us.
Only the chimney pots provided a link with a more prosperous railway age.
(G.Adams/M.J.Stretton coll.)

MP Middleton Press

EVOLVING THE ULTIMATE RAIL ENCYCLOPEDIA

Easebourne Lane, Midhurst, West Sussex.
GU29 9AZ Tel:01730 813169
www.middletonpress.co.uk email:info@middletonpress.co.uk
A-978 0 906520 B- 978 1 873793 C- 978 1 901706 D-978 1 904474
E - 978 1 906008 F - 978 1 908174

All titles listed below were in print at time of publication - please check current availability by looking at our website - *www.middletonpress.co.uk* or by requesting a Brochure which includes our *LATEST* RAILWAY TITLES also our TRAMWAY, TROLLEYBUS, MILITARY and COASTAL series

A
Abergavenny to Merthyr C 91 8
Abertillery & Ebbw Vale Lines D 84 5
Aberystwyth to Carmarthen E 90 1
Allhallows - Branch Line to A 62 8
Alton - Branch Lines to A 11 6
Andover to Southampton A 82 6
Ascot - Branch Lines around A 64 2
Ashburton - Branch Line to B 95 4
Ashford - Steam to Eurostar B 67 1
Ashford to Dover A 48 2
Austrian Narrow Gauge D 04 3
Avonmouth - BL around D 42 5
Aylesbury to Rugby D 91 3

B
Baker Street to Uxbridge D 90 6
Bala to Llandudno E 87 1
Banbury to Birmingham D 27 2
Banbury to Cheltenham E 63 5
Bangor to Holyhead F 01 7
Bangor to Portmadoc E 72 7
Barking to Southend C 80 2
Barmouth to Pwllheli E 53 6
Barry - Branch Lines around D 50 0
Bartlow - Branch Lines to F 27 7
Bath Green Park to Bristol C 36 9
Bath to Evercreech Junction A 60 4
Beamish 40 years on rails E94 9
Bedford to Wellingborough D 31 9
Birmingham to Wolverhampton E253
Bletchley to Cambridge D 94 4
Bletchley to Rugby E 07 9
Bodmin - Branch Lines around B 83 1
Bournemouth to Evercreech Jn A 46 8
Bournemouth to Weymouth A 57 4
Bradshaw's Guide 1866 F 05 5
Bradshaw's History F18 5
Bradshaw's Rail Times 1850 F 13 0
Bradshaw's Rail Times 1895 F 11 6
Branch Lines series - see town names
Brecon to Neath D 43 2
Brecon to Newport D 16 6
Brecon to Newtown E 06 2
Brighton to Eastbourne A 16 1
Brighton to Worthing A 03 1
Bristol to Taunton D 03 6
Bromley South to Rochester B 23 7
Bromsgrove to Birmingham D 87 6
Bromsgrove to Gloucester D 73 9
Broxbourne to Cambridge F16 1
Brunel - A railtour D 74 6
Bude - Branch Line to B 29 9
Burnham to Evercreech Jn B 68 0

C
Cambridge to Ely D 55 5
Canterbury - BLs around B 58 9
Cardiff to Dowlais (Cae Harris) E 47 5
Cardiff to Pontypridd E 95 6
Cardiff to Swansea E 42 0
Carlisle to Hawick E 85 7
Carmarthen to Fishguard E 66 6
Caterham & Tattenham Corner B251
Central & Southern Spain NG E 91 8
Chard and Yeovil - BLs a C 30 7
Charing Cross to Dartford A 75 8
Charing Cross to Orpington A 96 3
Cheddar - Branch Line to B 90 9
Cheltenham to Andover C 43 7
Cheltenham to Redditch D 81 4
Chester to Birkenhead F 21 5
Chester to Manchester F 51 2
Chester to Rhyl E 93 2
Chester to Warrington F 40 6
Chichester to Portsmouth A 14 7
Clacton and Walton - BLs to F 04 8
Clapham Jn to Beckenham Jn B 36 7
Cleobury Mortimer - BLs a E 18 5
Clevedon & Portishead - BLs to D180
Consett to South Shields E 57 4
Cornwall Narrow Gauge D 56 2
Corris and Vale of Rheidol E 65 9
Craven Arms to Llandeilo E 35 2
Craven Arms to Wellington E 33 8
Crawley to Littlehampton A 34 5
Crewe to Manchester F 57 4
Cromer - Branch Lines around C 26 0
Croydon to East Grinstead B 48 0
Crystal Palace & Catford Loop B 87 1
Cyprus Narrow Gauge E 13 0

D
Darjeeling Revisited F 09 3
Darlington Leamside Newcastle E 28 4
Darlington to Newcastle D 98 2
Dartford to Sittingbourne B 34 3
Denbigh - Branch Lines around F 32 1
Derwent Valley - BL to the D 06 7
Devon Narrow Gauge E 09 3
Didcot to Banbury D 02 9
Didcot to Swindon C 84 0
Didcot to Winchester C 13 0
Dorset & Somerset NG D 76 0
Douglas - Laxey - Ramsey E 75 8
Douglas to Peel C 88 8
Douglas to Port Erin C 55 0
Douglas to Ramsey D 39 5
Dover to Ramsgate A 78 9
Dublin Northwards in 1950s E 31 4
Dunstable - Branch Lines to E 27 7

E
Ealing to Slough C 42 0
Eastbourne to Hastings A 27 7
East Cornwall Mineral Railways D 22 7
East Croydon to Three Bridges A 53 6
Eastern Spain Narrow Gauge E 56 7
East Grinstead - BLs to A 07 9
East London - Branch Lines of C 44 4
East London Line B 80 0
East of Norwich - Branch Lines E 69 7
Effingham Junction - BLs a A 74 1
Ely to Norwich C 90 1
Enfield Town & Palace Gates D 32 6
Epsom to Horsham A 30 7
Eritrean Narrow Gauge E 38 3
Euston to Harrow & Wealdstone C 89 5
Exeter to Barnstaple B 15 2
Exeter to Newton Abbot C 49 9
Exeter to Tavistock B 69 5
Exmouth - Branch Lines to B 00 8

F
Fairford - Branch Line to A 52 9
Falmouth, Helston & St. Ives C 74 1
Fareham to Salisbury A 67 3
Faversham to Dover B 05 3
Felixstowe & Aldeburgh - BL to D 20 3
Fenchurch Street to Barking C 20 8
Festiniog - 50 yrs of enterprise C 83 3
Festiniog 1946-55 E 01 7
Festiniog in the Fifties B 68 8
Festiniog in the Sixties B 91 6
Ffestiniog in Colour 1955-82 F 25 3
Finsbury Park to Alexandra Pal C 02 8
Frome to Bristol B 77 0

G
Galashiels to Edinburgh F 52 9
Gloucester to Bristol D 35 7
Gloucester to Cardiff D 66 1
Gosport - Branch Lines around A 36 9
Greece Narrow Gauge D 72 2

H
Hampshire Narrow Gauge D 36 4
Harrow to Watford D 14 2
Harwich & Hadleigh - BLs to F 02 4
Hastings to Ashford A 37 6
Hawick to Galashiels F 36 9
Hawkhurst - Branch Line to A 66 6
Hayling - Branch Line to A 12 3
Hay-on-Wye - BL around D 92 0
Haywards Heath to Seaford A 28 4
Hemel Hempstead - BLs to D 88 3
Henley, Windsor & Marlow - BLa C77 2
Hereford to Newport D 54 8
Hertford & Hatfield - BLs a E 58 1
Hertford Loop E 71 0
Hexham to Carlisle D 75 3
Hexham to Hawick F 08 6
Hitchin to Peterborough D 07 4
Holborn Viaduct to Lewisham A 81 9
Horsham - Branch Lines to A 02 4
Huntingdon - Branch Line to A 93 2

I
Ilford to Shenfield C 97 0
Ilfracombe - Branch Line to B 21 3
Industrial Rlys of the South East A 09 3
Ipswich to Saxmundham C 41 3
Isle of Wight Lines - 50 yrs C 12 3
Italy Narrow Gauge F 17 8

K
Kent Narrow Gauge C 45 1
Kidderminster to Shrewsbury E 10 9
Kingsbridge - Branch Line to C 98 7
Kings Cross to Potters Bar E 62 8
King's Lynn to Hunstanton F 58 1
Kingston & Hounslow Loops A 83 3
Kingswear - Branch Line to C 17 8

L
Lambourn - Branch Line to C 70 3
Launceston & Princetown - BLs C 19 2
Lewisham to Dartford A 92 5
Lincoln to Cleethorpes F 56 7
Lines around Wimbledon B 75 6
Liverpool Street to Chingford D 01 2
Liverpool Street to Ilford C 34 5
Llandeilo to Swansea E 46 8
London Bridge to Addiscombe B 20 6
London Bridge to East Croydon A 58 1
Longmoor - Branch Lines to A 41 3
Looe - Branch Line to C 22 2
Lowestoft - BLs around E 40 6
Ludlow to Hereford E 14 7
Lydney - Branch Lines around E 26 0
Lyme Regis - Branch Line to A 45 1
Lynton - Branch Line to B 04 6

M
Machynlleth to Barmouth E 54 3
Maesteg and Tondu Lines E 06 2
Majorca & Corsica Narrow Gauge F 41 3
March - Branch Lines around B 09 1
Marylebone to Rickmansworth D 49 4
Melton Constable to Yarmouth Bch E031
Midhurst - Branch Lines of E 78 9
Midhurst - Branch Lines to F 00 0
Minehead - Branch Line to A 80 2
Mitcham Junction Lines B 01 5
Mitchell & company C 59 8
Monmouth - Branch Lines to E 20 8
Monmouthshire Eastern Valleys D 71 5
Moretonhampstead - BL to C 27 7
Moreton-in-Marsh to Worcester D 26 5
Mountain Ash to Neath D 80 7

N
Newbury to Westbury C 66 6
Newcastle to Hexham D 69 2
Newport (IOW) - Branch Lines to A 26 0
Newquay - Branch Lines to C 71 0
Newton Abbot to Plymouth C 60 4
Newtown to Aberystwyth E 41 3
North East German NG D 44 9
Northern Alpine Narrow Gauge F 37 6
Northern France Narrow Gauge C 75 8
Northern Spain Narrow Gauge E 83 3
North London Line B 94 7
North of Birmingham F 55 0
North Woolwich - BLs around C 65 9
Nottingham to Lincoln F 43 7

O
Ongar - Branch Line to E 05 5
Orpington to Tonbridge B 03 9
Oswestry - Branch Lines around E 60 4
Oswestry to Whitchurch E 81 9
Oxford to Bletchley D 57 9
Oxford to Moreton-in-Marsh D 15 9

P
Paddington to Ealing C 37 6
Paddington to Princes Risborough C819
Padstow - Branch Line to B 54 1
Pembroke and Cardigan - BLs to F 29 1
Peterborough to Kings Lynn E 32 1
Plymouth - BLs around B 98 5
Plymouth to St. Austell C 63 5
Pontypool to Mountain Ash D 65 4
Pontypridd to Merthyr F 14 7
Pontypridd to Port Talbot E 86 4
Porthmadog 1954-94 - BLa B 31 2
Portmadoc 1923-46 - BLa B 13 8
Portsmouth to Southampton A 31 4
Portugal Narrow Gauge E 67 3
Potters Bar to Cambridge D 70 8
Princes Risborough - BL to D 05 0
Princes Risborough to Banbury C 85 7

R
Reading to Basingstoke B 27 5
Reading to Didcot C 79 6
Reading to Guildford A 47 5
Redhill to Ashford A 73 4
Return to Blaenau 1970-82 C 64 2
Rhyl to Bangor F 15 4
Rhymney & New Tredegar Lines E 48 2
Rickmansworth to Aylesbury D 61 6
Romania & Bulgaria NG E 23 9
Romneyrail C 32 1
Ross-on-Wye - BLs around E 30 7
Ruabon to Barmouth E 84 0
Rugby to Birmingham E 37 6
Rugby to Loughborough F 12 3
Rugby to Stafford F 07 9
Ryde to Ventnor A 19 2

S
Salisbury to Westbury B 39 8
Sardinia and Sicily Narrow Gauge F 50 5
Saxmundham to Yarmouth C 69 7
Saxony Narrow Gauge D 47 0
Seaton & Sidmouth - BLs to A 95 6
Selsey - Branch Line to A 04 8
Sheerness - Branch Line to B 16 2
Shenfield to Ipswich E 96 3
Shrewsbury - Branch Line to A 86 4
Shrewsbury to Chester E 70 3
Shrewsbury to Crewe F 48 2
Shrewsbury to Ludlow E 21 5
Shrewsbury to Newtown E 29 1
Sierra Leone Narrow Gauge D 28 9
Sirhowy Valley Line E 12 3
Sittingbourne to Ramsgate A 90 1
Slough to Newbury C 56 7
South African Two-foot gauge E 51 2
Southampton to Bournemouth A 42 0
Southend & Southminster BLs E 76 5
Southern Alpine Narrow Gauge F 22 2
Southern France Narrow Gauge C 47 5
South London Line B 46 6
South Lynn to Norwich City F 03 1
Southwold - Branch Line to A 15 4
Spalding - Branch Lines around
Stafford to Chester F 34 5
Stafford to Wellington F 59 8
St Albans to Bedford D 08 1
St. Austell to Penzance C 67 3
St. Boswell to Berwick F 44 4
Steaming Through Isle of Wight A
Steaming Through West Hants A
Stourbridge to Wolverhampton E
St. Pancras to Barking D 68 5
St. Pancras to Folkestone E 88 8
St. Pancras to St. Albans C 78 9
Stratford to Cheshunt F 53 6
Stratford-u-Avon to Birmingham
Stratford-u-Avon to Cheltenham
Sudbury - Branch Lines to F 19 2
Surrey Narrow Gauge C 87 1
Sussex Narrow Gauge C 68 0
Swanley to Ashford B 45 9
Swansea - Branch Lines around
Swansea to Carmarthen E 59 8
Swindon to Bristol C 96 3
Swindon to Gloucester D 46 3
Swindon to Newport D 30 2
Swiss Narrow Gauge C 94 9

T
Talyllyn 60 E 98 7
Taunton to Barnstaple B 60 2
Taunton to Exeter C 82 6
Taunton to Minehead F 39 0
Tavistock to Plymouth B 88 6
Tenterden - Branch Line to A 21 5
Three Bridges to Brighton A 35 2
Tilbury Loop C 86 4
Tiverton - BLs around C 62 8
Tivetshall to Beccles D 41 8
Tonbridge to Hastings A 44 4
Torrington - Branch Lines to B 37
Towcester - BLs around E 39 0
Tunbridge Wells BLs A 32 1

U
Upwell - Branch Line to B 64 0

V
Victoria to Bromley South A 98 7
Victoria to East Croydon A 40 6
Vivarais Revisited E 08 6

W
Walsall Routes F 45 1
Wantage - Branch Line to D 25 8
Wareham to Swanage 50 yrs D09
Waterloo to Windsor A 54 3
Waterloo to Woking A 38 3
Watford to Leighton Buzzard D 45
Welshpool to Llanfair E 49 9
Wenford Bridge to Fowey C 09 3
Westbury to Bath B 55 8
Westbury to Taunton C 76 5
West Cornwall Mineral Rlys D 48
West Croydon to Epsom B 08 4
West German Narrow Gauge D 93
West London - BLs of C 50 5
West London Line B 84 8
West Wiltshire - BLs of D 12 8
Weymouth - BLs A 65 9
Willesden Jn to Richmond B 71 8
Wimbledon to Beckenham C 58 1
Wimbledon to Epsom B 62 6
Wimborne - BLs around A 97 0
Wisbech - BLs around C 01 7
Witham & Kelvedon - BLs a E 82 6
Woking to Alton A 59 8
Woking to Portsmouth A 25 3
Woking to Southampton A 55 0
Wolverhampton to Shrewsbury E4
Worcester to Birmingham D 97 5
Worcester to Hereford D 38 8
Worthing to Chichester A 06 2
Wrexham to New Brighton F 47 5
Wroxham - BLs around F 31 4

Y
Yeovil - 50 yrs change C 38 3
Yeovil to Dorchester A 76 5
Yeovil to Exeter A 91 8
York to Scarborough F 23 9